one Ordinary Hero

one Ordinary Hero

An autobiography

Janet Maker

Jane Thomas Press
Los Angeles

Snorkeling with penguins in the Galapagos, 2017

One Ordinary Hero

Published by Jane Thomas Press

Los Angeles, California
JaneThomasPress.com

Photo credit: p59 Leo Delati Photography

Cover illustration by: Roni Setiawan
Cover design by: Joanne Manzella

Book interior design by Joanne Manzella

Library of Congress Control Number: 2024904538

ISBN 978-0-9976619-3-4 (paperback)
ISBN 979-8-218-37447-1 (ebook)

Printed in the United States of America

For my grandchildren:
Mateo and Melody

Mateo and Melody at Santa's Village, 2023

CONTENTS

"The hero's journey always begins with the call. One way or another, a guide must come to say, 'Look, you're in Sleepy Land. Wake. Come on a trip. There is a whole aspect of your consciousness, your being, that's not been touched. So you're at home here? Well, there's not enough of you there.' And so it starts."

– Joseph Campbell

Me in the desert

Chapter 1

INTRODUCTION

"All the gods, all the heavens, all the hells, are within you."

– Joseph Campbell

This book started with a movie I saw called *Finding Joe,* which was about Joseph Campbell's myth of the hero's journey and how it applies to all of us. It made sense of so many things in my life that I wanted to write my story from that perspective.

I am in my 80s now, and I see that differences in how all of us have lived our lives show up very clearly in old age. I have numerous friends and acquaintances of more than 50 years duration, so I know a lot about how they have lived. When people are young, immersed in careers and family and looking toward the future, differences don't show up so clearly. But in old age, the results of our life choices become obvious. They run the whole gamut, from people who are doing nothing much, mostly waiting for death, to those who are still fully engaged in joyful lives.

For me, a critical point was an experience I had when I was 20 years old. I had read Aldous Huxley's *The Doors of Perception,* about his experience with psychedelic drugs, and I wanted to open my own doors. As an attractive and intellectually curious young woman, I was offered many things, and in due course I was offered psychedelics. I chose a safe person with some psychedelic experience, and we went off to the desert with peyote. I was apprehensive, but something inside was telling me that it was important for me to do this.

The desert is like a blank canvas—nothing much there except dry, bare earth with a few scrubby plants and a vast blue sky with a few white clouds—and peyote lasts about 12 hours. I didn't exactly hallucinate, but I did experience profound perceptual changes. I noticed that the world could look different ways, ranging from beatific and heavenly to hideous and hellish. Eventually it occurred to me that possibly the difference wasn't coming from outside; maybe it was coming from inside. Maybe what I was perceiving in the world reflected what I was thinking and feeling. Since I had plenty of time, I experimented. I changed my thoughts and emotions, focusing on either fear or love, and sure enough, the colors, the shadows, the clouds changed from threatening to friendly, and back again. The outer world changed to match my inner world. This was in the 1960s, way before Oprah and *The Secret,* so the idea that we create our own lives was completely new to me. But I realized even then that I had discovered the secret of life. The changes would not be so obvious when I was not on psychedelic drugs, but my personal reality would still correspond to my thoughts and feelings, and this meant that I had some control over my experience. I didn't know exactly what to do with this insight, but I never forgot it, and it gave me the courage to face challenges that I might have avoided, since I knew now that the reality of those challenges depended largely on how I chose to perceive them.

Joseph Campbell said that we are all called to do hard things, whether those things be slaying a dragon, writing a book, or building a business; and how we respond to those calls determines our lives. He thought that most people turn away from those challenges because of fear. In my case, my peyote experience had given me a way to handle my fear. I didn't always step up, but I stepped up a lot. Pretty much everything I'm proud of in my life involved confronting fear: getting my Ph.D.; teaching; writing books; adopting two children as a single parent; making money; traveling all over the world, often by myself.

When I read other autobiographies, they don't generally mention the fear, so I thought successful people didn't have any. My friends think I'm fearless about things I've done too. Here is the truth: no matter how many challenges I face, the fear doesn't end. What is different is that I know from experience that I am capable of handling the fear, so I don't usually let it stop me. I think that most things worth doing lie outside our comfort zones. Doing hard things is how we grow, and growth gives our lives purpose and meaning.

But living a good life isn't only about growth; it's also about morals. For example, all those tech billionaires have courage, and they are obviously growing their skills, but most of them don't seem to have any moral compass. I think a good life requires a second set of skills, centering on kindness and generosity. The Golden Rule, treating others as we would want to be treated, has been part of every religion, every culture, for millennia, and yet people still don't follow it. The part that seems to be too hard for most people is that our kindness and generosity must apply to everyone, whether or not we think they deserve it.

For most of my life, I was judgmental and critical when people behaved in ways that I disapproved of, just like my family was. Then, one day I realized that nobody deserves criticism under any circumstances. Some do need boundaries, but that can be done with kindness too. Refraining from criticism is an act of love, and as soon as I stopped criticizing people, my life became happier because I started spending more time in a state of love.

But to this day, even though I don't criticize people, I still find myself making judgments about others, as well as about myself. In order to stay on top of my fears and my judgments so they don't control my life, I have to constantly monitor my thoughts and emotions, and this is what I consider to be my most important work. I have been attending a weekly meditation group for about 30 years, and that helps keep me on track. We spend an hour together silently monitoring our sensations, responses, thoughts, and emotions. I have developed a habit that when I take my dogs for their daily walk, I try to use the time to observe myself instead of getting lost in my inner chatter. It's a lot of work, but it feels important because I believe it to be the foundation for everything.

I hope that readers will benefit from my experience and find value in this book. But if not, my daughter says that when I get too old to remember who I am, her kids will read me my book so I can remember who I was. That works, too.

Baby Janet

Chapter 2

CHILDHOOD

"That step, the heroic first step of the journey, is out of, or over the edge of your boundaries, and it often must be taken before you know that you will be supported."

– Joseph Campbell

I said that peyote changed my life, and it did. But there was something there first; otherwise, I would never have read Aldous Huxley or taken peyote. Most middle-class young American women didn't do either of those things, although they were becoming more popular.

I was always a seeker, and I can't really say why. Maybe I was just born that way. Maybe everyone is born that way and some people suppress it. Maybe it has to do with upbringing.

My mother provided a negative role model; at an early age, I realized that I did not want to be like her. She was very critical of everyone, always convinced that she was right and everyone else was wrong. She was not able to see me, her only child, or anyone else, as individuals with our own ways of living; my mother's aim was to dominate. I could see that this need for domination was caused by a deep insecurity, probably as a result of her own upbringing, but she was never willing to explore any of that. As a result, she alienated her family and had no friends, ending up as a bitter old woman, still blaming everyone but herself. Despite everything, I loved my mother, and I felt her pain. Although I wouldn't sacrifice myself, I did everything else I could think of to make her happy, but nothing worked.

My father was critical and judgmental too, but he was a better parent because he was more mentally stable, and he had a stronger moral core.

With my mother in Massachusetts, where I was born

Although he often criticized me, and I can't say I felt loved and appreciated, I knew he would not abandon me, and he had a sense of justice that I could appeal to. He told me that my mother was mentally normal when he married her, and he stayed with her for 22 years, before she finally divorced him. I was a teenager when they divorced, and they both sued for custody. My mother was impossible to live with, but in the 1950s most courts would not award custody of a girl to a single father. I was advised that I needed to say that I would run away if the court made me live with my mother. Although this was actually true, saying it in court in front of my mother was awful.

Suing for custody cost my father a lot emotionally and financially, and I will always be grateful to him for making that sacrifice for my sake. If not for him, I can't imagine what would have become of me. He also encouraged me to go to college. He suggested I study English, so that in case something happened to my future husband, I could make a living as a secretary.

With my father during WWII, when he was stationed in Washington, DC

After my father got custody, things did not always go smoothly. My father had a somewhat authoritarian personality, which made me rebel. When I was around 16, he became enraged for some reason, and pulled my phone out of the wall and told the manager of my part time job that I quit. It was spring break, so I was not in school, and I felt that my dignity required that I leave home. I knew an older girl who was on her own and who wanted company. We were living in the San Francisco Bay area during the height of the Beatnik era, and she suggested we go to North Beach. We checked into a fleabag hotel and went to jazz clubs. I had a great time. I knew the police were looking for me, so when my money ran out after a couple of weeks, I let them catch me. They put me in juvenile hall, which was also fun. All the cool kids were there, and they played great music on loudspeaker. I knew that they would not send me home if I said I would run away, but I felt sorry for my father, so I went home. He had contacted the school counselor, who agreed to mediate conflicts between us, so things improved. The irony is that, 30ish years later when I had teenagers of my own, a new thought popped into my mind: "I wonder if I did something to make him angry."

I'm in the back row between my mother and father at the wedding of my mother's brother.

I had always thought of my family as three people with nothing in common, thrown together by fate. However, recently, in my old age, I had an epiphany about my father. I realized that in many ways I am just like him. Maybe he was my inspiration. I had been so busy concentrating on our differences that I had never noticed our similarities: We are very motivated by intellectual curiosity. We are rigorous about telling the truth and keeping our word, including punctuality. We love travel, new experiences, and good food and drink. We have the same sense of humor. My father did hard things that must have taken courage. After WWII, he went to college at night on the GI bill and graduated Phi Beta Kappa in four years while working full time and raising a family. When he was 60ish, he was married to a wealthy woman, and he felt his manhood threatened. So, he made $10 million by investing on margin in computer stocks.

I'm in the middle row, 4th from the left

Although my father died in 2009 at the age of 99, I still talk to him. He doesn't talk back, and of course I have no way of knowing if there is anything that hears me, but it gives me comfort. If I think of anything I wish I had said before he died, I say it now, and that works for me.

In front of the legendary Checkerboard Lounge, Chicago

One other important thing happened in my childhood: At around the age of 12, I developed a lifelong passion for blues music. I first heard rockabilly and rhythm and blues, and I quickly traced it to its roots. All the blues greats were still alive at the time—Muddy Waters, Little Walter, Howlin' Wolf, and many more. I got a false ID so I could see artists live in clubs. We moved to Los Angeles in my senior year of high school, and the clubs I particularly remember were the 5-4 Ballroom at 54th and Broadway, and Moore's Swing Club in Compton, where T-Bone Walker regularly played. In that very segregated era, I had never really been around black people before, and the music and the dancing had me enchanted. This was the 1950s, and many of the white girls who frequented black clubs were prostitutes. So, I was offered money and I was not offended, and nobody was offended when I turned it down. People would invite me to parties, and I would go, and nothing bad happened. I started to make black friends.

Later I went to Chicago to all the clubs and met everyone. I knew someone who was a booking agent for blues acts, and she took me everywhere. One high point was Little Milton's birthday party. It was huge, all the blues musicians were there, and everyone took a turn on stage. Between blues singers they had shake dancers, which I guess is, or was, a Chicago thing. Massively obese women, very scantily dressed, dance, and the amount of shaking that occurs is breathtaking.

Shake dancer at Little Milton's birthday party, Chicago

Over the years, I have seen blues artists all over the world, and I still have blues streaming in my car every day. When I go on a road trip, I crank up the blues, sing and talk to myself, and by the time I arrive at my destination it feels like my soul has been cleansed.

When I was 80 years old and psychedelics had become more

or less legal again, I wanted to explore my fear of death, so I took psilocybin (mushrooms). I discovered a connection between my fear of death and the blues. My love of blues started before the civil rights movement, so the circumstances of some blues artists were not much different from slavery. Nevertheless, they were able to create beauty and joy despite their circumstances. Although comparing my life with theirs sounds ridiculous, at that time I had a similar lack of agency because I was a child. I got the idea that life is basically horrible, that the universe is uncaring and possibly malign, but that by an effort of will, I could create beauty and joy for myself. This actually worked out pretty well, but I ended up with the fear that when I no longer had the strength to fight, I would be left with the horror. After the mushrooms showed me the reason for my fear, I could start to move on from that belief.

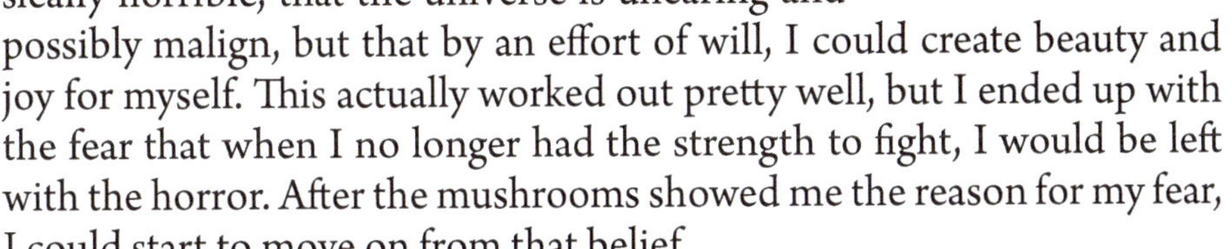

With Koko Taylor

With Albert King

With Albert Collins

In Los Angeles, 1965

Chapter 3

YOUNG ADULTHOOD

"The big question is whether you are going to be able to say a hearty yes to your adventure."

– Joseph Campbell

When I was old enough for college, my father's employer transferred him to New York. I could either stay in California, where the university was basically free (I believe it cost $72 per semester in 1959) and my father would help with room and board, or I could go to New York with him, but I would have to live at home because the universities there were expensive. I didn't want to live at home any more, so I ruled out New York. I was a Merit scholar and had qualified for nominal scholarships throughout the country, but to get serious money I would have to prove financial need, which I could not do. So, I opted to go to UCLA and live in a dorm.

Living on campus felt like a therapeutic experience for me. Dorms at that time were single-sex, and living with other girls who were more or less normal felt healing. I had normal friends from high school, and some of them are still part of my life, but I had never before lived in an environment that felt healthy. I had either lived with my disturbed mother and her bad marriage or with my father who didn't understand me. When I was a senior in high school, he got remarried to a wife with whom I felt no connection, and it was pretty clear that she could not wait for me to leave.

Although I had rejected my mother's way of living, early conditioning runs deep. I found myself with some of her suspicion of people, and my primary emotion seemed to be righteous indignation. Living with normal girls helped me to straighten out a lot of that, although I still had to monitor myself for many years. My relationships with men were harder. I was good looking, so I attracted a lot of interest, but I had no skills. My parents were not role models, so I tried to act the way people acted in movies. I was inauthentic and did not know how to ask for what I wanted. I would suppress my feelings until they finally erupted, sometimes justifiably, sometimes not.

I am grateful that I arrived in college just as the era of sexual freedom was beginning, but I had no clue how to handle any of that. At least I could talk with other girls, and I bumbled along. I did a lot of drinking and tried all the recreational drugs. I never had a drug problem, but drinking did become an issue. It never interfered with school or work, but sometimes when I drank, I would be going along fine and then all of the sudden I would be in a blackout and do reckless things like driving. It was very fortunate that I never injured anyone. I was stopped by the police several times, but never arrested. Once they had me walk a line (this was before breath tests) but because I had been studying ballet, I could do it even though I was very drunk. I had a friend who was not very drunk but who hit a kid on a bicycle. He didn't do any damage, but they threw the book at him. I had other friends who had to be bailed out of jail, but none of that happened to me. I continued with my issue for decades until it finally went away by itself, sometime around menopause. I don't know why it went away, but in the 30 years since then, my drinking has been completely normal. I imagine it was some kind of metabolic change.

So, between my lack of relationship skills, my drinking issue, and my obsession with blues, I was a handful.

I had worked part time during high school and college, and after my junior year I was able to pay for a summer session at the University of Mexico in Mexico City. I found a place to stay in the home of a middle-aged couple. The husband was a newspaper editor from Chile, and the wife was the consul from Panama. Her primary job was social, so she was always giving parties for visiting Central Americans, to which I was invited. I acquired a handsome boyfriend from Costa Rica and had a wonderful time until the end of the summer, when I came down with hepatitis. I fell in love with the Spanish language and with much of Latino culture. I read Spanish and Latin American literature, learned some poems and songs, and the following summer I went to Europe and spent most of my time in Spain.

After I returned from Mexico, I got a new boyfriend, a law student at UCLA, and it was with him that I went to Europe the summer after I graduated. Because of my aforementioned issues, and I imagine he had some too, we never got along very well, but we decided to get married anyway. I can't speak for him, but I had no idea what a good marriage looked like, so it would have been hard to hold out for that. When our marital discord became severe, we went to a marriage counselor, but he just told us to break up. I think that was a missed opportunity, because he might have helped us develop some skills, whether or not we ultimately stayed together. Later I was told that most marriage counselors should really be called divorce counselors, because very few of them actually help couples stay together. I think my ex and I were married for three years. We never reunited, but we did remain friendly until he died.

I had graduated with a degree in English, not so I could become a secretary as my father had recommended, but because I loved literature. At that time, the professions that were open to women were mainly teaching, nursing, and social work, and I didn't think I would like teaching or nursing. Anyone with a bachelor's degree could take civil service exams—federal, state, county, and city—and if you passed, you would be offered a job when your number came up. When my number came up, I was offered a job as a county social worker. My job was an intake worker for people, mostly families, applying for assistance. Most people needed temporary help because of some kind of disruption, such as an illness, a layoff, or a marital breakup. They just needed tiding over until they could get on their feet again. A smaller number would need permanent help because they fell into one of four categories, which we unkindly labeled as Sick, Stupid, Crazy, and Old. They would never be able to work again. At that time, we had no appreciable homeless population, I suppose because we provided help. We were not exactly compassionate; our applicants were treated with contempt, and I now feel ashamed about my role in that. But they were not starving or homeless, and they got some kind of medical care. When I hear about making America great again, this is what I think of. It wasn't great, but it was better.

This was the 1960s, and there was money for social improvement. A stipend was made available to all county social workers: If we wanted to get a master's degree in social work at any accredited institution, the county would pay our tuition and living expenses for the two-year program. We would have to return in the summer and work, and we would owe them another year of work after graduation. I viewed this as a great opportunity, and I got myself accepted at the Columbia University School of Social Work, which was then located in the Carnegie mansion on Fifth Avenue in New York. I had a friend from college who would be attending the NYU Institute of Fine Arts, and we agreed to get an apartment together. My father, who had gotten divorced, would house us until we found a place to live, which we did pretty quickly. One of New York's highlights for me was the Apollo Theater in Harlem and various blues venues. My roommate loved the art scene in Greenwich Village. We did a lot of dating of course, and I think the only thing that made us unhappy was the weather. The first snowfall was glorious, but then winter just kept dragging on, and on, and on. Finally, we took my roommate's student loan check and flew to Puerto Rico for Spring break.

In Los Angeles, 1960s

When I graduated, my roommate stayed to work on her Ph.D. I had enjoyed my two years in New York, but really, I preferred California. It wasn't only the weather; it was the convenience of being able to drive up to a grocery store and put my groceries in the car; and it was not having to take the subway, where it seemed that all kinds of smelly people had their hands either on my body or in my purse. But New York had great beauty and great art too, and I was grateful for my time there.

Later, when my father was married to his third wife, and after he had made his $10 million, I visited regularly and was treated to the best restaurants, the best theater tickets, and no subways. I have to say that California cannot top that. Luckily too, that wife and I liked each other, and we had a happy relationship until she died.

After I returned from New York, I owed LA County a year, which I spent as a child welfare worker in community protective services. I would investigate complaints of child abuse or neglect and decide what to do. Since that was a more compassionate time, we spent some energy trying to keep families together, and the county was willing to spend some money too. For example, if the home was filthy and the children were malnourished, I was able to send in a housekeeper to teach the family how to run a household if that seemed warranted. We could get them some assistance with parenting skills, so they would know what to do instead of smacking their kids. We only took the kids away as a last resort.

In England, 1968

The most lasting benefit to me from that job was a lifelong friendship with a mom from the community who was assigned to help me. She was a black mother with six kids, and we remain good friends to this day. She is 90 now, and a great-great grandma. She is a wonderful person, and we both love blues.

After my year was up, I got a job as a psychiatric social worker at the UCLA Neuropsychiatric Institute. My job was to work with the families of children hospitalized on the Child Inpatient service. I had high hopes for that job, but over time it became more and more disappointing. They operated on the medical model of mental illness, which meant that problems in living were given medical diagnoses and treated as illnesses. Of course, that approach wasn't very successful, and I didn't like being a part of it. Also, I had no kids of my own, and I really did not feel like an expert on parenting. Although I always received excellent job evaluations, I didn't feel that I was doing an excellent job. I lasted there for five years, and after I left, I had nightmares for years. In the dreams, I was forced to go back to work there temporarily for some reason, but nobody there believed it was temporary. They thought I had failed.

While I was still working there, I learned that I could become a school psychologist, which would at least give me summers off, and I would not have to work with any psychiatrists unless I called them in. There was only one part-time program locally for that credential, and it was at USC. USC is a private school, not cheap like UCLA still was at that time, but UCLA would not accept part time students, so I had no choice. I signed up for a course at USC called Diagnosis of Reading Disabilities. The professor was very well known in her field, and she ran the USC Reading Center, which trained teachers by working with kids with reading problems. She knew that I had never been a teacher and didn't know anything, but I was apparently the only student who followed directions and turned my work in on time, so she offered me the job of Coordinator of the USC Reading Center. That part time job would give me free tuition and a salary, and I could quit social work forever. That's also when I decided I might as well get a Ph.D.

With my father on a cruise to Bermuda, 1970s

I got other jobs as well. Lawyers would call the Reading Center looking for someone to determine such things as whether a defendant was able to read his Miranda waiver. In these cases, the police would say that the defendant had waived his rights, such as the right to remain silent and to have an attorney present, but there was doubt about whether he knew what he was waiving. These cases would be referred to me and I would have to testify in court. I was also asked to rewrite documents to make them readable. One was the voluntary sterilization agreement that

LA County Hospital had been using to sterilize women who had no idea what they were signing and couldn't understand why they weren't getting pregnant. Of course, readability was only part of those issues, but I was glad to participate. It was interesting.

While working at the Center, I became friendly with another student who was working on getting her Ph.D. in a related field, but who also wanted to get a reading specialist credential. She had friends who had started a small publishing business, and she invited me to create some educational materials with her that her friends would publish. I think we may have had to pay them. We did publish some things, but we had a hard time marketing them. We were able to turn some of them into a workbook, and another small publisher published that, but it only brought in a tiny sum.

Me at Bryce Canyon, Utah

Meanwhile, my friend met the English editor at Prentice-Hall, which was a top publisher of educational materials, and she tried to pitch him on our work. He told her they were discontinuing their elementary/secondary division, but they needed a textbook for college reading and study skills. He invited us to submit a proposal. We worked very hard on the proposal, and eventually we got the contract. My friend had most of the creative ideas, and I had most of the writing skills, so we made a good team, but writing the book was very difficult. If we had not had a contract, we would never have persevered.

As a bit of background: Prior to around 1960, only the elite typically went to college. But times changed, and it started to become necessary to have at least some college training in order to get a good job. As a result, poorly educated Americans started going to college for the first time. All the colleges had to institute programs for basic skills, especially in reading, writing, and math. We had gotten in on the ground floor of a new trend.

The next thing we knew, the other top publisher of educational materials, Wadsworth, approached us and asked us to submit a proposal for another kind of textbook for college reading. We got that contract too, and between the two companies we published seven textbooks which stayed in print for up to six editions, lasting about 30 years. Eventually, we made a decent amount of money, but not right away.

It occurred to me that I needed financial independence, so that I would not have to depend on either a husband or a job for money, in case either one mistreated me. I read some books, and it seemed to me that the best thing I could do was invest in income property. I didn't have much money, and I could only afford to buy in low-income areas. Because of my experiences in blues clubs and in Mexico, I wasn't afraid of minorities. But those properties were a lot of work. My tenants were the first people to lose their jobs, and I had a lot of evictions. I had to battle with roaches. The law required on-site managers for properties of a certain size, and I needed them anyway, to deal with the day-to-day hassles. However, those managers lived with my tenants, and I had to spend a lot of time on site to prevent them from being co-opted. But financially I got very lucky. During the 1970s there was an inflationary surge, and everything skyrocketed in value, including my properties. I could buy something, make no improvements, and quickly sell it for a lot more. I began teaming up with friends so we could buy more, and by the time the inflation ended, I had a tidy emergency fund. But I was burned out, and I lost my taste for income property. I did a few projects with friends after that, mainly at their instigation, but my heart wasn't in it.

My job at the Reading Center was a teaching assistant position, not intended to last forever. I spent a couple of years there, but I had to get another job, and by that time I knew I wanted to teach at the college level. I had started teaching mainly for the challenge. I had a public speaking phobia that was starting to interfere with my life. I did not want to go through life with a handicap like that, so I sought out opportunities to practice. This led to teaching, and to my surprise I found out that I was a born teacher. I felt that I did an excellent job, and it made me happy.

I was able to cobble together enough part-time teaching jobs to support myself, but getting full-time work was very hard. There had been a big hiring spree in the 1960s, and those hires had not yet started retiring, so the number of permanent job openings was close to zero. However, I was supporting myself well enough from teaching part time, and I had my emergency fund, so I had time to wait.

With friends in Yosemite. I'm on the left, 1973

Tommy and Jane, 1987

Chapter 4

MIDDLE AGE

"If you can see your path laid out in front of you step by step, you know it's not your path. Your own path you make with every step you take. That's why it's your path."

– Joseph Campbell

For my fortieth birthday, I threw a big party with a Middle Ages theme. My invitation showed a Joan of Arc-looking figure, wearing armor and wielding a sword, going to battle with a huge dragon who was labeled with things like middle-age spread, baldness, and flatulence.

I started thinking about having a family. I was not infertile so far as I knew, but my first choice was adoption. This was the 1980s, and I could foresee even then that all our lives were likely to end with nuclear holocaust and/or climate collapse. I did not feel justified in bringing new life into that, especially when there were so many orphans needing homes. I had other reasons, too. I didn't trust my genetics. I didn't know to what extent my mother's mental health issues were inherited, but I was afraid to take a chance that I could produce a child with her problems. Also, through my work as a social worker I had seen a lot of abnormal children, so I wanted to see what I was getting before committing myself. And I liked the idea of avoiding childbirth. I was born right after Pearl Harbor, and my mother told me that all the anesthetic was sent overseas, so she had labored with me for 72 hours with no anesthetic. I got the idea that childbirth was painful and dangerous. Finally, although some billionaires are denying it now, overpopulation was a major problem, and I didn't want to contribute to it. I felt fortunate that I didn't have a spouse who insisted on replicating himself, so I could make the decision that was best for me.

Although I would be older than other new moms, this was good timing for me. I was old enough so that anything I had failed to achieve in life, I could not blame on my kids for holding me back. I had already had my share of sex, drugs, and rock and roll, so I didn't feel my kids could deprive me in that department either. I had finally purchased income property in a reasonably good area, and I was living there and managing it myself, so I had stability. And I had my emergency fund. I did not have a permanent job, but I had my Ph.D., book royalties, rental income, and as many part-time teaching jobs as I could handle.

I started with the traditional adoption agencies, but I quickly learned that I was a victim of prejudice against single parents. They would only give single parents children who were handicapped or part of a family group, in other words, children that couples didn't want. There were some very expensive lawyers who would place ads to locate pregnant women and try to broker a deal, but I didn't trust them. I needed to screen the birth parents myself. Also, I thought that responsible birth parents would want to screen me. Just because they are relinquishing a child doesn't mean they don't care what happens to it.

This was before the Internet, so I looked in the yellow pages under Adoption. Along with the regular agencies, I found a small ad from the Universal Life Church. This was an organization that for a fee would send documents ordaining you as a clergy member, or even documents canonizing you as a saint. Some time back, I had become a Universal Life minister myself, and I officiated at the marriages of several couples who were friends of mine at lovely, unorthodox celebrations.

I called the number, and it turned out to be one guy who, for a $200 donation, would match pregnant women with potential adoptive parents. I sent the donation. I received several calls and met several women, but either I didn't feel comfortable with them, or else they wanted a two-parent home for their baby. Eventually I met a young woman who was willing, and I was willing, and we made an agreement. She had gotten pregnant accidentally and could not pay for an abortion. She already had one child, Donald, who was 3 ½ years old, and she felt that her limited resources could not be stretched far enough for two children.

At this moment, as I am writing these words, I am on a family cruise in the Caribbean to celebrate my son Thomas's 40th birthday, along with his biological half- brother Donald, my daughter, her husband, and their two children, my grandkids.

So, it worked out OK, but it was rocky for a while. Tommy's birth mother was already eight months pregnant, so things happened fast. We had agreed that it would be better to have no contact between my son and his birth family until the age of 18. I just remembered all the adolescent identity crises, and I thought it would be best to avoid complicating things. She wrote a letter for me to give to him when the time was right. Since she could not work, we agreed on a reasonable sum of money to tide her over.

On Tommy's birthday cruise, 2023
Standing: Donald, Tommy, Jane and Melody, Mike.
Sitting: Me and Mateo

I went to a lawyer, and we signed legal documents allowing me to take him home from the hospital and to provide medical care. When I got him home, I contacted the Bureau of Adoptions to begin the process. Once he was in my home, they could not turn me down just because they didn't like single parents. They would need an actual reason, such as a criminal record. The adoption process would take about a year, and during that time the birth parents would have the right to take the child back if they changed their minds. They wouldn't even have to give a reason.

The birth mother did end up threatening me and extorting more money, but she said she was desperate and had no other options, so I forgave her. It caused me some anxiety, but I was pretty sure she really did not want to take him back, so I felt that I had the option of calling her bluff. This is one reason I wanted to meet the birth mother myself rather than leaving it in the hands of a lawyer. Also, the total money wasn't that much, certainly nowhere near the sum I would have had to pay to a lawyer for arranging a match.

I hired a young woman named Zoila from El Salvador, and together we figured out how to take care of Tommy. She spoke no English, but I spoke some Spanish, so we managed. She stayed with me for a couple of years until she had her own unexpected pregnancy. Many years later, her daughter contacted me on Facebook and said her mother often talked about me and how I had helped her. I was happy to see that Zoila's daughter had graduated from college and seemed to be living a good life.

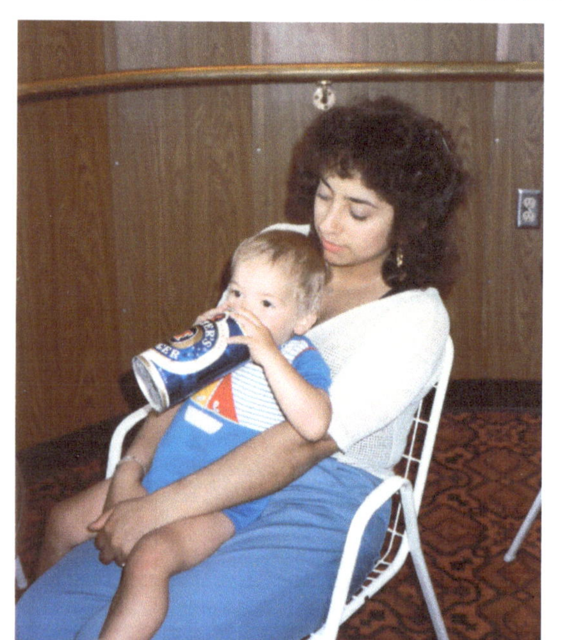
Tommy with Zoila, 1984

After Zoila, I had several different Hispanic housekeepers who provided childcare, cooked, cleaned, and did the laundry. Some were better than others, but really all of them were fine. Actually, the whole system worked wonderfully. It gave me the freedom to work, date, see friends, have a life. The housekeepers had the weekends off, and since the housework was already done, we just did fun activities all weekend, usually with other families. We lived next to UCLA, so when my kids were old enough not to need much help, I got UCLA students, usually from China, to stay in the house and keep an eye on things in return for free rent and utilities. That worked out fine too.

When Tommy was around two, I started looking to adopt a second child. I had been an only child, and I didn't want that for my son. I was hoping for a girl this time. Although amniocentesis was possible, it was not common, and I could not insist on it without jeopardizing the adoption. I decided that, although I wanted a girl, another boy would be OK.

I went back to the Universal Life Church, and eventually found a pregnant couple living in Phoenix. Tommy and I flew there to meet them. They seemed nice, and they had identical twin girls, 5 ½ years old.

They explained that the twins had been born prematurely at great physical and financial cost. They were just recovering from that, and really did not want another child. They told the twins the truth about their plans for their sibling, which I respected. We all hit it off, and we agreed on the adoption and on the amount of money I would be contributing to cover their medical bills. Because the girls had been born by Caesarean, this one would be a Caesarean too, so we would know the birth date.

When the time came, my father went with Tommy and me to Phoenix, and we met the parents and the twins again before the mother went into the hospital. After the birth, I met with her in her room, and we thanked each other. She was happy for me that it was a girl and confessed that the doctor had told her it would be a boy because he said he saw a penis on the ultrasound. I don't know what he saw, maybe a thumb? I named her Jane, after my father's deceased third wife. I think that if there is anything of her spirit left, it would be pleased to have a namesake, especially since she never had children of her own. It pleased my father, too.

Tommy holding Jane, 1986

I had the same Bureau of Adoptions worker for my second adoption. She said she had handled over 1000 adoptions in her career, and never once had she heard of any other adoptions through the Universal Life Church.

As my kids grew, I knew they would be asking questions about their families, and I wasn't sure how to answer them. I had read something by an expert on adoptions, so I paid for a one-hour phone consultation. She told me to truthfully answer any questions they ask, and when they turn 18 or leave home, whichever comes first, I should then tell them everything else I know.

That advice worked beautifully for us, when they asked if they grew in my tummy, when they asked if they had a daddy, and everything else. There were no secrets and lies, so there was no shame. I bought them books about how people have all different types of families—two moms, two dads, living with grandparents, single parents, foster parents, and adoptive parents. I don't believe they thought our family was odd. Eventually, they learned that they had biological parents and siblings, and that

Tommy and my father in Jackson Hole, Wyoming, 1984

I would help them connect with them when they turned 18, but not before.

There were, however, a couple of indications that Tommy might be having some issues with his adoption. When he was about five, we were in the car and out of the blue he said, "She gave me up because she wanted a better baby." We talked about it, and he seemed to feel better. The other time I remember was when he was about 15. We were having dinner, and he said that he had a feeling that he shouldn't do anything in life that would surpass his birth family. We talked about that too, but I sometimes wonder if that thought, even if it was subconscious, may have held him back.

While Tommy's adoption fantasy seemed to center on rejection, Jane's was the opposite. She said that she had pictured a conveyor belt with babies, and me looking for the perfect one. I picked her, and she felt chosen.

Tommy and my father in New York, 1984

My father was now a widower, and he spent a lot of time with us after Tommy was born. We visited him in New York, he visited us in California, and we went on lots of trips together, around the United States and in the Caribbean. My father encouraged me to buy a big house, partly because he wanted to live with us when he got too old to take care of himself. The house was a stretch for me financially, but my father would be there if I needed help. At that point, my father met his fourth and final wife.

She was very critical of me and of my kids. There was never a confrontation, but there was tension. She got my father to change his will, not in her favor because she had plenty of money of her own, but to leave his money to my kids instead of to me. And I was stuck with a big house that we loved but that was hard for me to afford. We have all heard fairy tales about evil stepmothers—Cinderella, Snow White—and it happens in real life too. It happened to one of my friends. She was an only child, and her father left everything to his new wife instead of to her. Another of my friends, happily married to the same man all her adult life, specified in her will that her share of the community property was to go to their children rather than her husband, because she feared that if she died first her husband would remarry someone who would get him to disinherit his kids. Apparently, this is something that men but not women do.

My father and his wife had moved from New York to Palm Beach, and he became more and more estranged from us. Then his wife had a stroke, and my father hired a team of nurses to care for her at home. Sometime later, the nurses found my father unconscious on the floor and called an ambulance. They called me, and I brought the kids to visit him in the hospital. He would never walk again; he was incontinent, and he had some dementia. The nursing team expanded to take care of both my father and his wife.

At that point, his wife was no longer capable of doing any harm. Any kind of communication was hard for her, so we resumed our visits and our relationship. We also developed a good relationship with the nurses, who disliked the wife's family. Eventually my father amended his will. His estate had been depleted by all the nursing care, but it was still too much money for young people to have.

With Tommy and my father

My father's wife died, and he remained an invalid for around 15 years, dying when he was 99. He had always loved to travel, but the only way he could travel comfortably now was on cruises, bringing two nurses with him. So, we went on lots of cruises, all over the Caribbean, and occasionally in the north Atlantic and Europe. Cruising turned out to be perfect for our family. There were activities on board for all age groups, and we came together for meals. We hired a guide with a wheelchair van for excursions in each port. I also snorkeled in pretty much every place in the Caribbean that has good snorkeling. Now that I am old, I can still snorkel because there is no gravity in the water. The only difficulty for me is getting back on the boat. I even had occasional problems with this when I was younger. On one excursion maybe 25 years ago, the group went to the snorkel location in a rubber inflatable boat. We jumped off and snorkeled, and everyone got back on except me. The sides of the boat were too high and I just could not do it. The guys running the boat reached down to pull me on, but that didn't work either. They had to get in the water and push on my rear end until I flopped over the side of the boat. I had a similar experience mounting a horse in the Dominican Republic, but at least I wasn't wearing a swimsuit.

In Carlsbad, New Mexico, 1981

In the 1990s I finally got a permanent job. Los Angeles Trade Technical College, part of the Los Angeles Community College District, was in danger of losing its accreditation because students were learning their trades but then failing their licensing exams. The accreditation committee required them to hire a reading specialist to set up a program, and they hired me. I set up a testing program which would slot students into classes that were high, medium, and low, based on their reading levels, and I also taught those classes. This was great for my textbooks because I could test everything on actual students. Most of my part-time teaching had been for teachers learning how to teach reading. This was the first time that I was actually able to use my own books.

The lowest classes were for people reading below sixth grade level. Some students could barely read at all, including the textbook for my class. I arranged for them to have access to the blind reader, which was in the library. You put the book face down on the machine, and it reads it to you aloud. We also had a budget to buy practice materials to keep in a lab inside the library, and I bought graded materials starting at first-grade reading level but at adult interest level, so my students would not be subjected to kitties and puppies. My classes were graded Credit/No Credit, so I did not have to assign letter grades. I would not assign credit based on their progress, because better readers progress faster than poorer ones. So, I graded them on whether or not they completed the homework in the textbook and all the lab work.

We met once a week in the classroom to go over the material in their textbook and once a week in the lab, where I would meet with them individually to monitor their progress on the graded lab materials. There are certain reading skills that must be taught at every level, such as identifying main idea and supporting details in paragraphs and eventually in longer selections. If they could do it at one grade level, they would move up, working until they mastered the skills at the new grade level. I was actually surprised at how well this worked. I would have thought that students with such low reading levels would have complicated dyslexic or intellectual issues, but this was not the case. They just needed a teacher. I don't know what had happened to them. Maybe they were sick during a crucial period in elementary school and fell behind. Maybe they moved to a different school district that was too far ahead. Maybe they had early dyslexic issues that later resolved. When children have reading problems, they tend to try to hide the problem and avoid reading, which makes everything worse.

On Alaska cruise with my father, just before Tommy was born, 1983

I couldn't help noticing that some students did not do their homework. I started harassing them, and what happened next opened my eyes. Since we met individually in the lab, some of them would tell me their reasons. One of them had a brother who was just shot. Some of them were homeless. I got the message, and I stopped judging.

I remember one student who had been so hurt by his early experiences with reading that he could not bring himself to do the work in my class for fear of failure. He sat through the whole class without receiving any credit. But apparently his trust levels increased, because he came back the next semester and did his best. I had promised my students that if they did the work they would receive credit, but some of them had a hard time believing me.

My work was fulfilling, and the thing that made it more so was the level of gratitude that I received. When people can read better, it's a big deal to them.

Students in the medium-level classes were reading around junior high school level. They had basic literacy, but they were not able to handle college textbooks, which meant that they had trouble in their classes. As well as increasing reading levels by teaching basic skills like main ideas and supporting details at different grade levels, we also went into specialized information about how to read textbooks and study for tests.

In Paris, 1987

Students in the high-level classes were reading at high school level, so they still needed some help in reading college textbooks and studying for tests. We also went into reading efficiency, how to read as quickly as possible without losing comprehension. And we covered critical reading. Critical reading and thinking is not hard to teach, and it can actually be taught at medium and low levels as well as high. You start by making sure you understand both points of view (or more if there are more than two); then you identify the evidence supporting each point of view, and figure out which evidence is more convincing. This is something Americans are shockingly bad at doing. For example, whenever our government wants to get involved in another war, they simply tell us that they are doing it for the sake of democracy. Since they don't want citizens to consider the opposing point of view, they tell us that the leader of the other side doesn't have a point of view—he is simply crazy. It doesn't matter whether it's Saddam or Kim or Putin, or whoever is next; they are all supposedly crazy. It shocks me to my core that Americans never fail to fall for something so obvious, but they always do. Clearly, US schools are not teaching critical thinking. This may be intentional, so that citizens can be more easily manipulated.

At Trade Tech, I went to the administration and offered to present workshops for faculty, to teach them how to help their students understand the material they were teaching. It would be a simple matter of preparing study guides, introducing difficult concepts and difficult vocabulary before students had to read them, etc. Not too hard, but faculty did not seem to be willing, which was really too bad for the students.

I remained at Trade Tech for 12 years and retired when I was 62. In all my working years, from my twenties to my sixties, I always had a decent salary and great benefits: excellent health insurance with no co-pay, sick leave, vacation time, sabbaticals, and generous pensions. Sadly, most working people don't have those benefits anymore. I guess I was born at the right time.

At a dude ranch in Arizona with my kids, 1988

At the Mount Kenya Safari Club, standing on the equator. My father and Zoila were babysitting Tommy, 1985

Tommy, Jane and me, 1988

Chapter 5

TOMMY & JANE

"Your life is much deeper and broader than you conceive it to be."

– Joseph Campbell

Jane was born when Tommy was three years and five days old. I thought this was an ideal age difference. They were close enough in age to bond with each other, but Tommy had settled down enough by that age so that I could take the two of them places by myself without too much trouble.

Jane was an easy child. If they were all like her, I could have raised six of them—until adolescence. Tommy, on the other hand, was a firecracker. In a way, I felt sorry for him that he had me as his mother. He might have been happier in a large family that loved sports and games instead of living with a mom who loved reading and writing. This is an argument for adopting older children when their personalities are already evident, so you can get a better match.

In any case, I loved him a lot and did my best to accommodate his activity level. We both loved travel, and we did a lot of that, starting in his infancy. I had summers off, as well as breaks in winter and spring, and we went everywhere. On shorter breaks we usually visited my father when he lived in New York and in Florida, and he came with us on visits to national parks, to resorts, and on cruises. Tommy's adoption wasn't final until he was a year old, so I had to get some kind of special permission, in addition to his passport, to take him out of the US, and later I had to do the same thing for Jane, but it wasn't a big problem.

In summers, we would usually go somewhere for at least a month. The summer that Tommy was three and Jane was an infant, we went to Paris. I brought a UCLA student and paid for her trip in return for her help. I reserved two reasonably priced rooms with fridge and microwave in a hotel almost next to the Louvre. During the summer, there was a small amusement park set up in the park in front of our hotel, and if he behaved himself, Tommy would end each day with one ride of his choice. Since Jane didn't have teeth yet, we had to buy French baby food, which was interesting. They didn't have little jars labeled "strained beef" like we do. The French jars contained things like strained filet of sole sauté meunière. Jane got lucky.

Tommy was not only extremely active; he was also extremely independent. In the airplane on the way to France, he asked me if he could see the cockpit. This was before 9/11, but we were already in the air, so I didn't

Tommy in Paris

With Tommy in Paris

think it would be possible. Jane was on my lap and I didn't want to go, so he asked if he could try. He came back saying "Come on—we can see it." So, I bundled up Jane, and when we arrived at the first-class section, the flight attendant stopped us. I said that my son told me we could see the cockpit. She said, "But he already saw it, with his father." Apparently, Tommy had picked up some guy and got him to accompany him into the cockpit.

Tommy in Paris

Tommy had been recently toilet trained, and he developed a fascination with French plumbing, which was actually interesting in its fantastic variety. Since I was usually occupied with Jane, he would go to the men's room by himself, and sometimes he got so absorbed in his plumbing explorations that I had to find a man to go in and retrieve him.

His favorite French story, one that he still loves to tell, is about the time when he asked me to hold his French pastry and made me promise not to eat it. I did promise, but whatever he was doing took a long time and the pastry was calling to me, so I broke my promise. When he discovered my betrayal, he went stomping down the street, shouting, "I'm angry!"

A friend of mine from Los Angeles visited us with her young son for part of the time, and we took day trips all over Paris and the surrounding areas. We went to all the museums, and I took pictures of the kids in front of the great works of art, hoping that these photos would instill in them a love of art. It didn't work.

The next summer we spent a month in Rome. A friend of mine had friends living in Rome who would be away for the summer, so I could rent their apartment, complete with a male Ethiopian housekeeper and a very Italian dining area outside under a grape arbor. I got another UCLA student, and off we went.

Tommy never walked when he could run, and right away he face-planted in the Roman Forum. Blood was pouring from the vicinity of his eye, and I could not tell how seriously he was injured. I found a carabiniere, who drove us at breakneck speed to urgent care. Turned out the injury was no big deal—that part of the body just bleeds a lot. He had a cut over one eye, but they sewed it up and told us to come back on a certain date. We did go back, and that's when I found out what is wrong with American health care. They asked me if I worked in Italy or had a relative who did. I didn't, and they apologized, but they would have to bill me the full cost. That turned out to be the equivalent of $16, less than the taxi fare to the hospital.

Tommy and Jane in Rome

For me, the part of Rome I think I loved the most was Ostia Antica. The name means "ancient mouth" because the city had been a port at the mouth of the river Tiber during ancient times. The harbor started silting up during the second century, and the city of more than 100,000 inhabitants had been abandoned. It was an easy Metro ride from central Rome, and we loved to picnic there. They had what in Italy is called a bar, and I could order cold beer and delicious Italian sandwiches. The ancient buildings were still standing, with their mosaics and statuary, and everything was accessible. It was a fabulous place to explore.

Another place of interest to both kids and adults was Monte Testaccio. This had also been a port on the Tiber in a different location in ancient times. Ships would unload there, and they threw the broken pottery into a huge pile estimated to contain about 53 million amphorae. The pile is still there, and we were allowed to help ourselves to it. I brought home some ancient pottery that is still displayed in my family room.

Whenever we went to a new country, I would teach the kids how to say please, thank you, hello, goodbye, and count to ten in the local language. For months after her return from Rome, Jane's hello and goodbye was still ciao.

Tommy and Jane in Capri, Italy

With Tommy in Jamaica

The summer when Tommy was six and Jane was three, we spent a month in Costa Rica. We stayed with a family in a suburb, and I attended a language school while the kids attended a local preschool. Neither the family nor the school spoke any English, and the kids picked up enough Spanish so they could at least ask for things they wanted.

Tommy and Jane at preschool in Costa Rica, 1990

It was in Costa Rica that I discovered the value of personal injury lawyers. Here in the US, we think of them as pond scum, but their value becomes clear in places that don't have any. I had signed us up for an excursion to see sea turtles lay eggs. This would be at night, and they told us not to bring flashlights, and I foolishly obeyed. It was a wild beach, covered in driftwood. We found a big turtle and watched her dig a nest, lay her eggs, and leave. But when it was time for us to leave, the tide came in, and the sand more or less liquefied. My legs sank in up to my hips. Jane took off running, and Tommy grabbed the hand of the guide, leaving me to flounder in the dark.

On the Jungle Train, Costa Rica, 1990

Another time we took what was known as the Jungle Train, which was a wonderful ride through the jungle and on high trestles across raging rivers. The problem is that the train regularly went off the tracks, and the crew would have to get out and put it back on.

Another time, we went on a horseback expedition. Jane's horse decided to take advantage of having a three-year-old rider by eating grass instead of keeping up with the group. I was not a great rider myself, but I had to go back and round them up, because the leader wasn't going to do it.

Americans traveling abroad trust that they will not be offered activities that could be unsafe, because that's true at home, but it's definitely not the case where there are no personal injury lawyers to ensure accountability.

We didn't get into any serious trouble, but we could have. Another group of tourists was climbing on a nearby volcano when it erupted, and the tourists were killed.

Horseback expedition, Costa Rica, 1990

We also did domestic trips. The one thing that the US has that is as good as anywhere on Earth is our parks system, and the variety of our geography. One summer I needed to meet with an editor in Oregon. We brought a friend's daughter who was in between Tommy and Jane in age. I packed up the three kids and our two dogs, and we did a road trip up the coast to Oregon and back down through the California national parks, including spending a glorious week in a houseboat on Lake Shasta. Another summer we did a road trip through the national parks and Indian ruins in Arizona, New Mexico, Colorado, and Utah.

When Jane was four and Tommy was seven, I remarried. Before the kids were born, I had gone to New Orleans, partly to present a paper at the annual convention of the International Reading Association, but mainly to attend the New Orleans Jazz and Heritage Festival. I met a man there, and he made occasional trips to California for business, so we would get together from time to time over the intervening ten years or so. He called and invited me to Mardi Gras. I was very stressed and depressed at the time, because of problems with my father due to his fourth marriage, plus financial problems related to having such an expensive house, and I also had a 54-unit apartment building in Fresno that had asbestos contamination. So, I thought Mardi Gras would be a good idea. He and I got carried away, and we decided he would move to Los Angeles and we would get married. I was in desperate need of emotional support, so I ignored all the red flags that were waving furiously. He was a lot of fun, and he cheered me up and helped me get through the rough patch, but it couldn't last. The main problem for me is that he did not tell the truth and keep his promises. He just said whatever he thought would make his life easiest at the moment. I didn't want to live with that, and we broke up after about three years. My children were very hurt, and I blamed myself. I could have easily foreseen what would happen if I had been in my right mind. We did not keep in touch, but when I was 80 years

Tommy and Jane in New Orleans, 1989

old, he contacted me on Facebook. I didn't reply because my memories of him were not really happy, and I imagined he was probably looking for someone to take care of him in his old age.

After my second marriage broke up, I felt so guilty that I stopped dating. When my kids were old enough that they didn't care anymore, I found that the dating pool had dried up. Also, I had learned something from my experience, and I didn't want to hang out with men who I didn't respect, so that narrowed the dating pool to pretty much zero.

Tommy was happy in preschool, but when he got to regular school where they expected him to sit still and pay attention, he didn't do well. He didn't fail; but he was not really happy with the school, and the school was not really happy with him. He had to be kept busy, so he joined everything that was available: every sport in every season, chess club, drama club, tennis, golf, swimming, scouts, literally everything he could find. He had a short attention span for those things too, but our rule was that once he signed up for something, he had to finish it, and he did.

Tommy and Jane

Jane and Tommy in New York

Tommy and Jane

One advantage of adoption is that the children can have talents that the parents don't have. I can't carry a tune, and when Tommy was born, friends said that since he wasn't mine, maybe he would be musical. It turned out that he had perfect pitch, and when he was old enough, he joined a boys' choir at his school. He had a very loud, shrill speaking voice. If there was a birthday party of 30 kids, Tommy's voice could be clearly heard, and one of my friends mentioned having fantasies about cutting and tying his vocal cords. So having that voice finally channeled for a good purpose was rewarding. The choir trained for around eight hours a week, traveled to various events to perform, and even appeared on the Jay Leno show. Jim Carrey was also on the show, and he ended up wrestling with the boys on TV.

Tommy as a choirboy, 1993

The school recommended medication for ADHD, so I took him to doctors and got prescriptions for various drugs. Tommy did not like the meds and would not take them voluntarily. I had to physically watch him swallow the pills or he would spit them out. I did that, but when I asked the teachers if they noticed any difference, they said no.

Although ADHD causes a lot of problems, it also has upsides. Tommy's eagerness to try new things and his fearlessness made him a lot of fun to do things with. I really enjoyed his company. Jane says that Tommy helped her, too. His adventurousness pulled her out of her shell and got her to try things she would have been afraid to do without him.

In 1992 there was an earthquake in Big Bear Lake, a mountain community about 100 miles from where we lived. It was a fun place, with hiking and boating in the summer and skiing and snowboarding in the winter. There was a small year-round population, as well as a lot of vacation homes owned by people in Los Angeles and San Diego. Lots of owners were freaked out by the earthquake and were selling their properties, which created a unique buying opportunity that I found irresistible. I found a charming cabin that had been divided into two 2-bedroom units.

The back unit I rented out on a monthly basis, and the front unit I put on vacation rental when we weren't using it.

We kept that cabin for more than 10 years. We used it for boy scouts, girl scouts, silent auctions at the kids' schools, and lots of family vacations. We would often bring friends for Jane and Tommy and sometimes for me. It was close to the ski lifts, and the kids learned to ski and snowboard, but I really preferred summers. My favorite things were hiking in the mountains and puttering around the lake on rented pontoon boats. The lake was cold and not great for swimming, but I would bring an ice chest with picnic food and beer for the adults, pack up the kids and dogs and sometimes some friends, and it would be a lovely few hours. I sold the place at a big profit after my kids grew up, and I returned to Big Bear for the first time just this year. We rented a large house, with room for Tommy, Jane and her two kids, Jane's biological sister and her two kids, and me. We had a great time, and I think my favorite thing was the pontoon boat.

Girl Scouts at our cabin in Big Bear

Jane with dolphin in Hawaii

Jane did better in school than Tommy did. She was a good student, but her real gift seemed to be social. She was extremely good at making friends and knowing the right thing to say in every situation. I was asking her advice about things like thank-you notes and difficult conversations when she was still pretty young. She was also good at sports, especially softball and cross-country running, but she did not pursue extracurriculars with the energy that Tommy did. When her friends would come over to play, they would frequently stage dramas. One that I recall was called "The Sleeping Booty." Apparently, the princess's rear end had fallen asleep and could only be awakened by a kiss from the prince, who was played by our dog. I enrolled her in a program at Santa Monica Playhouse, and she took part in several productions there, but by the time she reached middle school she did not want to participate in school dramas because she did not want to be on stage in front of her peers.

The deterioration of my kids in adolescence broke my heart. Tommy had never been completely honest, but I could no longer trust anything he said. Jane, who had been trustworthy all her life, was following Tommy's lead. We went to various family counselors, but none of them helped. Just at that time, a new high school opened up that traveled, and Tommy was able to spend ninth and tenth grades there. It was a local school, but they went on a one-month domestic trip in the fall and a two-month foreign trip in the spring. In ninth grade, the fall trip was to the Pacific northwest and the Spring trip was to southern Africa, where they toured and camped and also did homestays. The curriculum was geared to Africa: they studied African geography, African literature, and the foreign language was

Traveling in Africa while my father and Zoila were babysitting Tommy, 1985

Zulu. They performed a dance for the queen of Swaziland, and they were present at Nelson Mandela's final address to parliament. Jane and I went to South Africa to meet up with Tommy when his school trip ended. We toured on our own where he had already been, starting in Cape Town, and we picked him up in Johannesburg. From there, the three of us went to various game parks and to Victoria Falls in Zimbabwe, where Tommy bungee jumped off the Zambezi bridge. We had a great time.

Tommy at Dodger Stadium

The following year, the fall trip was to the southwest US, and the spring trip was to China, where they toured and also did homestays and attended school in Beijing. Tommy was happy with the school, and the school seemed happy enough with him, but unfortunately the director of the school discovered that her husband of 35 years had another family on the side, and she moved to North Carolina. So that was the end of the school. There really wasn't any other school that was a good fit for Tommy. By that time, he had started stealing and doing drugs, and I was not able to monitor him closely enough to keep him safe and out of trouble. So, I hired a consultant who specializes in these things, and he ended up going to a boarding school in Maine for 11th and 12th grade, and Jane followed a year later when she was in 9th grade. Unfortunately, when Tommy turned 18 in 12th grade, he decided to leave school. I would not let him come home or send him any money, because he had the option of going back to school. He preferred to be homeless in the Boston area until he managed to get a job at Abercrombie & Fitch. Eventually he got a GED and started college in various places, but he never finished. He came home and went to community college for a while, but I kicked him out when I caught him stealing.

Jane and Tommy as teenagers

While he was at home, his birth mother called. When he turned 18, I had given him the letter she wrote to him before he was born, but he did not reach out to meet her. After she called, he went to Minnesota to meet his birth family, which by that time also included a younger half-brother.

Tommy with his younger half-brother Montana, 2005

Tommy met a girlfriend in Minnesota who he lived with for a time. She went on some cruises with us when my father was alive. She also spent some time with Tommy in California, and I visited and met her family in Minnesota. That went well, but eventually Tommy's dishonesty ended that relationship, and also the relationship with his next girlfriend. To make a long story shorter, Tommy was a very late bloomer. He has been stable and doing well for a few years now. I asked him to explain the change, and he said that he always knew the difference between good and bad, but he wanted to experiment with the bad and see how that would work. He decided he was happier being good. I have more questions I want to ask, but one step at a time.

He works as a property manager in northern California, a job that has a lot of responsibilities. I am extremely pleased that he is doing very well there. His employers must be pleased too, because they have promoted him. Tommy seems happy with what he has achieved and has plans for his future. He visits once a month, spending time with me and also with Jane's family. He helps me with whatever I need, and he is a big help to Jane, too. Her children adore him. He has been a good brother, a good son, and a good uncle for a while now, and my trust is slowly rebuilding.

Jane did not work out at the boarding school in Maine. She went from there to a wilderness program and then to a school in Utah. Because it was a year-round school, she was able to skip 11th grade, so she came home as a senior in high school at 16. I tried to find someone who could help us make sure her life at home was a success, and that's when we finally got lucky. A neighbor recommended an organization, and they assigned a case manager named Adam. Whenever Jane and I had a problem getting along with each other, Adam would solve it. If Adam had been in our lives years earlier, Jane would never have had to go to boarding school, and maybe Tommy either.

We discovered that, in order for Jane to graduate from high school, she needed one class that they were not offering that term. Adam arranged for her to take it at the local community college, and she went off to UC Santa Cruz when she was 17. Before she left, she asked me if I would help her contact her birth family even though she was not yet 18. I knew her birth parents' names and where they were from, so I started looking there. I found someone with the same name as her birth mother, and Jane called her, but the woman denied being her mother. We didn't believe her, but Jane wanted to pursue the matter because she knew she had sisters, so I hired a detective. We discovered that the woman with the same name was not the birth mother. The actual birth mother, who I had thought was very nice, turned out to be a sociopath, who fooled me as she had fooled many others. After Jane's birth, she had left her husband and, after many adventures, ended up married to a Texas zillionaire who adopted the twins. She manipulated her lesbian lover into shooting the zillionaire, and eventually both women ended up in prison. This story was on television, and if I had seen it I would have recognized who it was, but I never watched television during those years. There are also two true crime books written about it. The birth father committed suicide about 10 years after they broke up. The twins remembered that there had been a sibling who was adopted, but they did not have enough information to find her.

Jane (center) with her sisters Kristina and Jen at the Hearst Castle, 2012

Jane was of course upset by this information, as she had imagined her birth family quite differently, and she also had questions about heredity. She and her sisters arranged to meet. The sisters had had a lot of counseling, and they were able to help Jane. They were not sure that their father was actually Jane's father, but they did DNA testing, and they do have the same mother and father.

It has been almost 20 years since Jane met her sisters, and more than 20 since Tommy met his biological mother and two half-brothers. Although all family relationships have bumps, I would say that it has been a plus for everyone, including me. One of Jane's sisters lives fairly close by, in central California, with her husband and two daughters. We see them fairly often, and I have a lot of affection for them. Jane's other sister and Tommy's brothers live out of state, and we have a relationship with all of them.

Jane studied psychology and went on to become a behaviorist, working with children in schools and in their homes. Adam decided to go out on his own and start a business, and I was sure he would fail because he had no credentials, but as of now he has about 40 employees in offices in northern and southern California. After Jane had her own children, she began working for Adam part time, because she could adjust her hours to accommodate her kid's schedules.

Jane has the same values I have, so we pretty much agree about everything important. She is a great daughter, and I think she is doing an excellent job raising my grandkids.

Tommy, Jane and Jane's sisters Jen and Kristina at her graduation from UC Santa Cruz

Me with Jane's sisters

Me with Jane and Tommy at Hearst Castle

My father with Tommy, Jane and me at Disney World

Jane and me at her graduation from UC Santa Cruz

With Mike and Jane at their wedding, 2014

With Mateo, Jane's first baby, 2018

Tommy and Jane with Melody and Mateo as the Grinch and Cindy Lou Who, 2023

Melody (center) with her cousins Brooke and Ashley, 2022

Hiking with friends in Death Valley

Chapter 6

RETIREMENT

"When we quit thinking primarily about ourselves and our own self-preservation, we undergo a truly heroic transformation of consciousness."

– Joseph Campbell

After I retired, I thought I would teach some classes part time, and the school did call and offer them to me, but I had moved on. I had joined some new activities and made some new friends.

The first thing I joined was the Sierra Club. In Los Angeles we have the Santa Monica mountains, which are beautiful areas with many hiking trails. I joined a group called the moderate hikers, which were people around my age. We hiked once a week, usually around 4-8 miles, and we also became friendly and did some social stuff, as well as taking extended Sierra Club trips to national parks and other scenic areas around the country. When I look back on my life, I can only think of five things that have been extremely meaningful to me:

- Family and friends
- Career and achievements
- Blues
- Travel
- The outdoors

Maybe I should add food and drink, art and literature; but anyway, being outdoors on the trails was a big deal to me. I enjoyed the exercise and the companionship, but the main thing for me was the beauty of the environment.

I also joined a Spanish conversation group of intermediate-level speakers with a leader from Argentina, and we did some traveling together too.

By that time, I owned a place in Spain. After George W. Bush was reelected in 2004 with his war agenda, I got it in my head that he was going to reinstate the draft, then draft my kids and get them killed. My son had to register for the draft, and I imagined that a new draft would include girls as well. Both my kids were draft age. I remembered the Vietnam war very well, and I also knew that Bush had made a deal with Canada that they would not accept American draft dodgers this time like they had during the Vietnam era. That seemed ominous to me, and I felt that I had to do something proactive. I started going to Quaker services, because Quakers are pacifists and I thought that might get my kids out of a draft. I actually liked the Quakers quite a lot. Their services were completely silent, and people only stood up and spoke if called to do so by God. If someone spoke for ego reasons, then one of the Quakers would take him aside and talk to him afterward. Also, they did not make decisions by majority rule because they thought that was too violent; instead, they would wait until everyone was in agreement. Very, very nice people. However, I learned that being a Quaker was no longer enough to qualify for conscientious objector status unless you had been a Quaker from birth, or something like that.

Tommy and me in Málaga

I thought that it would be a good idea to get out of the country. I would have chosen Mexico, but I didn't think things were stable enough for Americans there, and I decided it had to be in the EU. Within the EU, the countries with the most appealing lifestyles for me were Spain and Italy, but I had to rule out Italy because the prime minister at the time was Berlusconi, who was more right-wing than Bush. Spain had declined to join the pro-war coalition that Bush was building, so that gave me hope that they might shelter draft dodgers. I had always loved Spain anyway.

I researched a bit, and it seemed to me that the best place for me to live in Spain would be Málaga, a city of half a million inhabitants on the Costa del Sol, across from Africa. It's a cruise port and a cultural hub for the province of Andalucía, with more than 30 museums. I didn't recall ever having been there, but I went to see, and it lived up to my expectations. I thought I could be happy there. The coastline looks a lot like California, with a mountain range running parallel to the beach, except these mountains run east-west instead of north-south. The buildings and gardens have a grace and charm that those in California don't have, except for those that are Spanish style. I thought it was beautiful. At intervals along the beachfront were chiringuitos, outdoor seafood restaurants. In front, on the beach side, was something that looked like a boat but contained hot coals for grilling the fish. There was also a kitchen in the back. Lunch was served starting around 2 p.m. and they cooked whatever the fishermen caught that day. Everyone drank a lot of wine, sometimes followed by coffee and liqueurs, and then went home for a siesta. Sitting and looking at the Mediterranean, eating fresh fish, drinking and talking, and then taking a nap, was my idea of the absolute world's best lifestyle.

Paella near Málaga

I shopped around and found an apartment in a beautiful retirement community. The residents were mostly expats from various countries in northern Europe. My apartment needed to be gutted and remodeled, and I had always enjoyed decorating, so that was fun. Years ago I had fallen in love with the historic Arab baths in Spain, with their intricate tile work and ceiling vents in the form of eight pointed stars, so I had my main bathroom tiled and stars painted on the ceiling. My intention was to rent out my house in Los Angeles and live in Málaga until it became clear what the next step should be. I had my garage sale and even a bon voyage party.

I had some legal questions, but I had a very hard time finding a lawyer who knew how Spanish law would apply to American citizens. I was particularly concerned about inheritance tax, because my father was in his 90s. I needed to know what would happen if he died while I was a resident of Spain. I kept searching and getting referred to different American law firms that had offices in Spain, but it took months to find someone who knew. It turned out to be very bad. After the US took its cut, Spain would have taken most of the rest. I really could not become a resident of Spain while my father was alive. However, I could spend, if I remember correctly, six months a year there as a visitor. I decided to go every spring and fall and also use it as a launching pad for trips all over Europe, the Middle East, and Africa.

I would have liked to rent my apartment out when I wasn't there, but hard as I tried, I could not find anyone in Spain who would manage it as a rental for me, and I knew from my former landlord experience that for me to try to manage it myself from California would not work. Instead, I offered it free to all my friends for their use when I wasn't there, and quite a few of them took me up on it, which pleased me.

I had the apartment for 11 years and sold it before the pandemic, because I was getting too old to keep going back and forth. I never did become a resident of Spain even after my father died, because my kids were no longer draft age and because Spain was too far away from them. My apartment had not been a good financial decision because I bought it when the euro was very strong against the dollar and sold it when it was weaker. With the cost of maintaining it for 11 years, I probably lost some money. However, I gained a lot of other things.

I knew nobody in Spain when I started, so I thought about how to make friends, and I watched carefully to see how that process worked. First, you have to find enough in common so that you have things to talk about, and they also have to trust that you would not do or say anything shitty even if you were really upset. That seemed to be the bottom line. Things like values don't even matter that much. For example, there was a couple I got friendly with who had a right-wing hatred of various groups, especially Muslims. I have no respect for that at all, but I still had affection for the couple, and I think they felt the same way about me. I guess we could never be besties, but we could definitely go out and have fun together. I met others who did have values similar to mine and who had bestie potential. I learned that I could adapt to living in another country, another culture, without much trouble. Really, the only thing that bothered me was dealing with businesses. In the US, whenever a business mistreats me and I need them to do something, I write to the head of the company—the president or CEO—and I get what I want about 90% of the time. But Spain doesn't work that way. I was told it's based on who you know, and I didn't know anybody.

Another thing I learned about myself was how I had changed over time. There were places in Spain that I hadn't seen since I was there in 1963, at the age of 21. Some of those places really had not changed much, so changes in my perception of those places were likely due to changes in my personality that had taken place over the intervening 40+ years. I had been much more romantic and poetic when I was young than I am now. That's a loss in a way, but maturity has its value too.

I had some Spanish experiences that were especially beautiful and/or fulfilling. Here are some examples:

Semana Santa

Semana Santa, or Holy Week, is celebrated all over Spain. The one in Seville is the best, but the one in Málaga is pretty great too. Different brotherhoods maintain religious floats and carry them in daily processions. Each brotherhood has different colored elaborate robes and pointed hats like the Ku Klux Klan. I think that the Klan was inspired by the Spanish Inquisition. Tiny children whose dads belong to the brotherhoods wear tiny outfits to match. People watch from their balconies and some of them sing saetas, which are very beautiful religious flamenco songs. The night proces-

Semana Santa in Málaga

sions carry tall candles. By the way, António Banderas is from Málaga and belongs to a brotherhood there. He would take part in the processions, and you could sometimes see Melanie Griffith sitting on a balcony when he was married to her.

The Royal Andalusian School of Equestrian Art

The Royal Andalusian School of Equestrian Art in Jerez del la Frontera trains horses and riders. They have regular performances, in which the horses dance to Spanish music. Traditional Spanish riding garb doesn't look silly like the British. The riders look dignified and elegant, and so do the horses. It was like nothing I had ever seen, and its beauty made me cry.

Flamenco

Flamenco music can be lowbrow and made for tourists, or it can be profound and of great beauty. It touches some of the same emotional chords that blues does. When it's great, there is nothing better.

Spanish cowboy

April Fair

The April fair in Seville is a combination of horses and flamenco. The horses are dressed up very elegantly, with styled manes and tails, and paraded constantly all over the fairgrounds with handsome men wearing traditional garb in the saddle and beautiful women in flamenco dresses, or sometimes children, perched on the back. The fairgrounds are covered in rows of more than 1000 casetas, which are green or red-and-white striped tents of varying sizes arranged along 15 streets. In the streets and in the casetas, there are crowds partying and dancing sevillanas (a type of flamenco), eating, and drinking all night long.

Fighting Bulls

I went to a ranch that raised fighting bulls and also gave demonstrations. Spanish cowboys don't look like American cowboys. They wear outfits that are elegant, and they have perfect posture. Keep in mind that fighting bulls are very dangerous to people and to horses, so there is a very high level of horsemanship involved. The bulls are led into the arena by oxen and there are thrilling demonstrations of working with the bulls and feats of horsemanship. Some of the beauty and danger was reminiscent of bullfights, but I don't go to bullfights as a matter of principle. I probably shouldn't go to ranches that raise fighting bulls either, but at least there was no killing.

Islamic Architecture

Spain was ruled by Muslims for 700 years, which ended with their expulsion in 1492. The reconquest began in the north and moved slowly south, which was the part of Spain that remained under Muslim rule the longest. I have always thought that Islamic architecture is the world's most beautiful, and especially the architecture from that historical period. The best-known buildings are the Alhambra in Granada and the cathedral (formerly a mosque) in Córdoba. But the remnants of Muslim rule are all over Spain, especially in the South. The ruins of Medina Azahara, a fortified palace-city, are on the outskirts of Córdoba. Málaga has a Moorish palace, a fort, and baths. I have gone to the Arab baths in Córdoba several times, and they are otherworldly, with beautiful, tiled pools of different temperatures and the stars on the ceiling. There are a lot of Roman ruins in Spain as well, but I think the Moorish ones are more beautiful.

Molecular Cuisine

For about five years, El Bulli on the Costa Brava was rated the best restaurant in the world. It pioneered molecular cuisine, and it attracted both chefs and patrons from everywhere. I never ate there, but I did go there with some friends just to look at it after it was closed for the season. It was located above a cove, so I guess you can get there by boat, but we took the road, which was very, very long and had a lot of turns. I don't know how anyone got out of there at night after they had been drinking. Dani García, a chef who had trained at El Bulli, went from there to Marbella and opened a restaurant called Calima. Marbella is close to Málaga, so of course I went, several times. It was beautiful, and the tasting menu was astonishing. It had, I think, 12 small courses. The astonishing thing was that the food was not only delicious; it was also creative, witty, and poetic. For example, they made things that looked like one thing, say an egg or an olive, but turned out to be something else entirely. They had one dessert that was named after a nearby natural park. I went to the park the next day, and sure enough it looked like the dessert. There was a course that looked like a particular holiday that is celebrated in Málaga. Eating there was a magical experience.

With my high school friend Marcia at Calima in Marbella

Tapas

Then there were tapas. People do tapas crawls, because different places specialize in different things, such as seafood or ham. However, if you don't know what you are doing, tapas can be mundane and not very good. In Málaga, people have taken me on tapas crawls that were just great, but I was never able to replicate the experience because I could never remember the right places. When I was in Barcelona, I was not able to find good tapas on my own, but a local tour guide gave me the names of some places that still give me joy to recall.

Paradors

Paradors are historical buildings, such as castles, palaces, fortresses, convents, monasteries, and even a few modern buildings that the Spanish government has converted into hotel accommodations with appropriate interior design, and which also specialize in regional cuisine. There are nearly 100 of them as of this writing, and I have stayed in many of them. They are beautiful, and some of them make me feel as if I have been transported back in history.

There are other wonderful things in Spain that, sadly, I never got to see. There are festivals all over Spain, all the time. Possibly the best known to Americans are the running of the bulls in Pamplona and La Tomatina near Valencia, which is a food fight using tomatoes. I am too old for those, but there are dozens of others that I would love.

I miss Spain. The saddest thing about being old is that when you visit a person or a place, you know it will likely be for the last time. I doubt that I will ever have the chance to see the things I never saw in Spain, or that I will have a chance to re-experience the things I know and love.

After I retired, it was important to me to experience as much as possible of this planet—see the sights, meet the people, eat the food, hear the music. I deeply regret that there are places that are off-limits because of US military activity—Syria, Iraq, Libya —and even Iran seems unsafe now. I hate that I will most likely never see them. But I have seen a lot.

I would often travel with friends. I liked to plan very far in advance, mainly so I could use air miles for first-class upgrades. I have probably gotten between $100,000 and $200,000 worth of free air travel from using my credit card. But most of my friends didn't like to plan that far ahead. So, I would usually just make my plans, and either the friends would come or they wouldn't.

I have probably done about 50 cruises in my life. I have been pretty much everywhere that cruise ships go: Antarctica, the Arctic, different transatlantic routes, the South Pacific, the Adriatic, the Black Sea, the Baltic Sea, the Indian Ocean, Iceland and Greenland, the Mediterranean, the Persian Gulf, the Galapagos, and the Caribbean many, many times. There is nothing like drinking rum punches while listening to Caribbean music and snorkeling in that perfect water. There are also theme cruises, so of course I have been on blues cruises. And river cruises.

I have also been on pretty much all the cruise lines, from the top of the line to the bottom of the barrel. Some have better food and service than others, but the thing I care about most is the itinerary. People travel for different reasons. Some want to experience luxury; some want to meet the people. The thing I care about more than anything else is seeing new places.

I loved all my cruises, but the ones I found most interesting were those without Americans. In 2012 an Italian cruise ship, the Costa Concordia, sank in the Mediterranean. I sensed a bargain, so I checked the Costa website, and sure enough, prices were extremely good. So, I booked a cruise in the Persian Gulf—Dubai, Abu Dhabi, Oman, UAE. It was a regular size cruise ship—maybe 2500 passengers—but I discovered that I was the only American on board. I loved the cruise, and it turned out that I very much enjoyed being with people who were not American. So, I booked another Costa cruise, this one going from Italy to Brazil.

In the Persian Gulf

On both cruises, there were six official languages: Italian, Portuguese, English, French, Spanish, and German. We had assigned seating at dinner but not at breakfast and lunch. They tried to put language groups together at dinner and also on the excursion buses. But if your language was not one of those six, they put you with whatever group you understood best. So, the English-speaking buses often had very few native speakers, but were filled with Dutch, Danes, Turks, Croats, etc. Same with the dinner table. We could kind of manage at dinner, but for breakfast and lunch we had open seating, and I was often seated with people with whom I could not converse at all. I guess they have language apps now that could help.

All ship announcements had to be in all six languages—everything on the ship, even the dance classes. We had a lot of those, especially on the Italy-Brazil cruise, because Brazilians love to dance. I love to dance too, so I attended classes pretty much every day we were at sea. Most of the men I danced with did the typical male thing of not being able to keep time to the music and then blaming me. We were short of men anyway, so I decided to learn the male part so I could lead. I was quite popular with the single ladies because they had the same problem with the men that I had, but I usually ended up dancing with a particular Turkish woman. She and I danced well together, but we did not have one single word in common in any language.

Another thing about Brazilians, and the Europeans on the ship too, is that they didn't seem to have body shame like Americans do. As soon as we got into the hot weather zone, they appeared at the swimming pools in very scanty swimsuits, both men and women, regardless of age or shape. After I got over my initial shock and revulsion, I started to admire their freedom, and it even started looking kind of sexy in a weird way. There is nothing sexy about being ashamed of your body.

I dislike flying, so when I went to Spain, I always tried to go at least one way by ship. Once I was crossing the north Atlantic on the Queen Mary 2, on the route of the Titanic. I was at lunch, and a woman at our table recounted how she was on another Cunard ship, when in the middle of the night the alarms went off and the captain said, "This is not a drill. Get your life jackets and report to your muster stations." She got to her station, and she saw all the crew members getting into the lifeboats, apparently intending to leave the passengers behind. Ultimately, they put out the fire and nobody had to abandon ship, but in a real emergency, it would likely be everyone for himself.

I also took train tours, another place where Americans were absent. My first one was on a train called the Transcantábrico, because it went across Cantabria, in the north of Spain. It pretty much followed the pilgrimage route of the Camino de Santiago, traveling between Santiago de Compostela and León. In Santiago, before I boarded the train, I stayed in the beautiful parador, which had been a lodging for pilgrims in the 15th century, next to the famous cathedral. After I disembarked in León, I stayed in the parador there, which is considered one of the most beautiful Renaissance buildings in Spain. On the train, I had my own room with double bed and bathroom—small, but with everything I needed. We would have breakfast on the train every day, complete with wine and champagne because this was Spain. We would get off the train to see the sights

Me with the Transcantábrico

and have lunch and dinner in restaurants, focusing on regional cuisine. Alcohol was included of course, not only unlimited wine with meals, but digestifs and other liqueurs with coffee. I had to take proton pump inhibitors because of acid reflux, but it was so, so worth it. Nobody else on this tour was American, but everyone spoke either English or Spanish, at least as a second language. Highlights for me included Altamira, where we went in the replica cave, and Bilbao. I had been to Bilbao in 1963, when it was all covered in industrial soot. Now it was cleaned up beautifully and was home to Frank Gehry's Guggenheim Museum and a Calatrava bridge, both of which were pretty great, but I thought the museum was phenomenal. Unlike a normal museum, the architecture allows you to see the art from different angles, which was a revelation.

Palace on Wheels, India

Some of the people on the tour were very knowledgeable about train travel, so I asked them where else I should go. They said Palace on Wheels in India. So that was my next train trip.

Palace on Wheels has several itineraries in India. The one I took was a round trip from Delhi, and included Jaipur, Chittorgh Hill Fort, Udaipur, Jaisalmer, Jodhpur, and Agra, as well as a national park that had tigers. I had a bedroom and bathroom and a guy in uniform and turban to take care of me. The train traveled at night while we slept. We would have breakfast on the train, do our excursions including lunch, and then we would come back to the train for dinner, which was catered by local restaurants. Because this was not Spain, alcohol was not included, and the experience was less joyous. But it was very good. India can be both very beautiful and very shocking, and being cocooned in luxury helped with the shock. Later, I learned that the Transcantábrico had been purchased by Palace on Wheels. I'm sure they do a good job, but I fear that they may have removed the joy from the experience.

My next train trip was not so luxurious. My daughter's then-fiancé, now-husband, had a summer study program in Korea, so we all went there for a two-week tour, then Jane and I went on to Beijing, where we connected with the trans-Mongolian, trans-Siberian, and trans-Ural railroads from Beijing to St. Petersburg. Unlike the other train trips, which were like cruises in that you only unpack once, this one involved different trains. When we got off for excursions, sometimes lasting several days, we had to take all our stuff, and we got back on another train. We were with a tour company that arranged the whole trip, but our train accommodation was second class, which meant four to a compartment and a bathroom down the hall. Our bunkmates were a 40ish Canadian couple who we liked a lot, which was fortunate.

In Korea with Mike and Jane, 2013

In Mongolia we got to stay in a yurt and ride Mongolian horses, which was great, but Jane stuck her head out the train window and got something embedded in her eyeball. She could not continue that way, so we stood in line with all the Mongolians at a clinic in Ulan Bator. I couldn't look, but a girl pulled it out of Jane's eye with tweezers. When we got back to the US, the ophthalmologist said she did an excellent job.

Russia was very impressive. Traveling by train, you realize how vast it is, both in terms of area and in terms of history. We stopped at Lake Baikal, Ekaterinburg, Moscow, and St. Petersburg. I had seen St. Petersburg before, which is very, very beautiful, but I had never seen Moscow. Somehow, I was expecting Soviet-style apartment blocks, but central Moscow looks like a Russian fairy tale.

In Mongolia with Jane

My next train ride was worse. I was taking the Ghan in Australia from Alice Springs to Darwin. It was very overpriced, and there was only one night sleeping on the train, so I figured how bad could it be and foolishly reserved second class. The compartment had two single seats facing each other. At night, those seats become one single bed, and a shelf pulls down overhead to become a top bunk for a second person. I believe there was a sink, but the bathroom was down the hall. At some point after we started, a young Asian woman entered my compartment. She didn't speak English, but I gestured to show her the accommodation. She burst into tears and I never saw her again. So, I had the compartment to myself, but it was still awful.

I also took bus tours without Americans. For example, I took one in New Zealand that was all English speaking, but I was the only American. The other travelers were Australian, South African, Indian, Canadian, and British. The only problem for me occurred one night when we were returning from a Maori village and someone insisted that each nationality sing a song typical of their country. As the only American, I would be doing a solo, and I cannot carry a tune. In fact, when my children were young and they misbehaved, I would threaten to sing to them, and that would straighten them out right away. Anyway, I quaveringly began "Yankee Doodle" and thankfully some of them knew the words and joined in.

Me in Japan

I also traveled on my own without a tour, but only in places where it was fairly easy to do so, such as Europe and Australia. In Europe, I would usually rent a car, but in Australia I had arranged to be picked up and transported to different places. This was quite nerve-wracking when they didn't show up. Once I signed up for what I thought would be a guided tour in Croatia, but all the "tour" did was reserve the hotels and transportation, and I had to make the connections. I was with a friend, but she was older than I was and had some memory issues, so I was the one in charge. Things got off on the wrong foot when we arrived in Zagreb and the person who was supposed to pick us up never showed. Most of the other connections showed up eventually, but there were hotel mix-ups and other stressful things. I don't recommend that type of tour unless you have an extremely laid-back personality. The best part of the Croatia tour was a one-week cruise. There are many islands off the coast of Croatia, and some of them are little medieval jewels—very beautiful, with good food and drink. Our boat only had 40 passengers, and we could jump off the back and swim in the Adriatic.

Once I went on a guided tour of Japan with a friend, and then we visited Vietnam and Cambodia on our own. After we toured Angkor Wat, my friend flew home from Siem Reap. I was flying first class using air miles, and I could not get a flight back right away, but the airline told me that they had a flight from Phnom Penh a few days later. I agreed to do that, and I started looking for hotels. I found a bargain at Raffles, which is rated as one of the top hotels in the world, very deluxe. The price was good, I booked it, and they asked me if I wanted airport pickup for an extra charge, so I booked that too. When I arrived, I was met by a man in elaborate uniform, and he escorted me to an extremely impressive car with pennants flying from its fenders. When we got to the hotel, the staff was waiting outside to greet me. I felt like Mick Jagger. When Jane and I took our train trip, I had found a bargain at Raffles Beijing. I enjoy 5-star hotels when I can get a bargain, but for me they are not worth paying full price. I am happy with 4-star hotels. They are not dingy and depressing like 3-star hotels can be. The difference in price between 3-star and 4-star hotels is not great, and I think it's worth paying. But the difference in price between 4-star and 5-star hotels can be very great, and for me it's not usually worth it.

In Cambodia with author of a book about his experiences living through the killing fields

My son-in-law reminded me that any discussion about my travels must include my trip to Burning Man in 2015. He and my daughter had gone there for several years before they had children, and they felt strongly that this was an experience I should have. They went to great lengths to secure an RV with heat and a/c for my comfort. Unfortunately, just before I was due to go, I injured my spine by excessive horseback riding at a dude ranch in Wyoming. There was a morning ride and an afternoon ride, each lasting about 2 ½ hours in Grand Teton National Park. It was fabulously beautiful, and I had all kinds of plans to bring my family there, but apparently the impact of all that trotting was too much for my cervical spine. I was in great pain and could barely walk. Eventually I got an epidural injection that helped, but I wasn't in very good shape. My kids located a motorized wheelchair at Burning Man that we called "The Cheetah" because it had a spotted seat cushion, and I went. I was glad I did—they were right that it was an experience not to be missed. My favorite things were the art cars, although I also enjoyed quirky things like the naked skateboard park, as well as the music, fire dancers, and of course when they burned the man. The overarching themes of Burning Man are self-expression and a rejection of corporatism and capitalism, which I can appreciate.

Me and Jane with Mike as DJ at Burning Man

Art car at Burning Man

Mike with art car at Burning Man

In South Africa

In Morocco

In Madagascar with lemurs

With Jane on the Great Wall of China

In Switzerland

At Machu Picchu

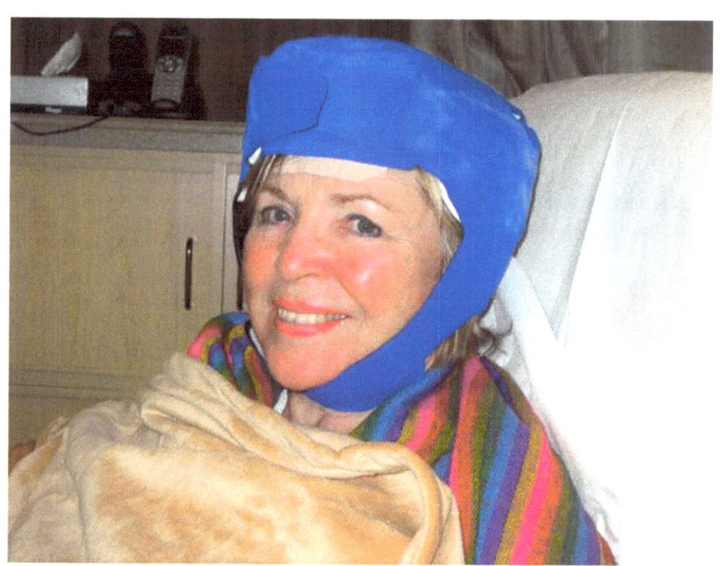

Wearing cold caps to save my hair during chemotherapy

Chapter 7

HEALTH

"We're not on our journey to save the world but to save ourselves. But in doing that you save the world. The influence of a vital person vitalizes."

– Joseph Campbell

In 2011, at the age of 68, I was diagnosed with breast cancer. It was found accidentally during a scan for something else. When I was in Costa Rica, I developed bronchitis which I couldn't seem to cure, and it eventually developed into bronchiectasis, a condition which is considered progressive and incurable. I went to many pulmonologists, including the Mayo Clinic in Minnesota, and nobody could suggest anything except surgical removal of one lung. I was getting more and more disabled, when I remembered something. When Jane was about four, she had something wrong with her voice that made her sound like the voice in *The Exorcist*. I was taking her to various ear, nose, and throat specialists (ENTs), and they were sticking tubes down her nose and torturing her, but nobody could find the problem. At that point, Tommy was in a boys' choir, and the choir director suggested that I take her to see the ENT who treated all the singers, because that doctor would have to be competent. So I did, and he told me that Jane's problem had to do with the size of her vocal apparatus. I should leave her alone and she would outgrow it and become completely normal, which is what happened. It occurred to me that I should go to that doctor. However, he had retired, and the choir director had also left.

By googling, I found the choir director in Oxford, England, and he told me who the new doctor in Los Angeles was who treated the singers. I went to him, he stuck a camera down my throat, and told me that my bronchiectasis was caused by esophageal reflux. He gave me a couple of prescriptions and sent me to a vocal coach. I improved by about 75% almost immediately, and I kept improving slowly after that, eventually achieving a 100% cure from a disease that pulmonologists considered incurable. However, the bronchiectasis had left some lung damage that took a long time to go away, and meanwhile it had to be periodically checked. It was on one of those scans that they saw something in the lymph nodes in my left armpit. I had had breast cancer scares before, and things had always turned out to be benign, so I wasn't particularly worried, and I went off with my family to celebrate Christmas in Venezuela. I know now that I should have viewed those previous scares as red flags.

In Venezuela with Jane, Mike, and Jane's sister Kristina

When I got my diagnosis, metastatic carcinoma, I didn't believe it. I thought they were wrong, especially since they couldn't find any cancer in my breasts, only in my lymph nodes. But I had test after test, and they all said stage 2 breast cancer.

Like most people, I knew very little about cancer, but whenever I have a big problem, my natural tendency is to seek information. I knew from my experience with ENTs and pulmonologists that I could not afford to just follow what my doctors told me. If I had trusted what the pulmonologists had told me, I would most likely be dead now. I joined a support group at my local Cancer Support Community, and I also got information online, especially at breastcancer.org. I told my friends that I had breast cancer, and gave them permission to tell anyone they wanted, and I got a lot of information from them.

I had to choose three, possibly four, doctors: a breast surgeon, a radiation oncologist, a medical oncologist for chemotherapy and hormone treatments, and a plastic surgeon if I would be getting breast reconstruction.

The first thing I had to address was surgery. I consulted five breast surgeons, but they disagreed about whether or not I would need a mastectomy, although they all agreed that I would need lymph node removal. Since they couldn't find any cancer in my breast, some of them wanted to amputate, just to be safe, and some of them even wanted to amputate both breasts, to be safer. A friend of a friend came up with the solution. She knew a radiologist who had a machine that was much more accurate than the equipment that regular radiologists use. I went to him, and he did very thorough imaging and biopsied two suspicious areas. He said that I probably had cancer in my breast at one time that was overcome by my immune system, but there was no cancer now. I asked what he thought about mastectomy as a preventive measure, and he said that there was no need for that; an annual MRI would be enough to tell me if the cancer came back.

However, I did get the lymph node surgery, which was probably unnecessary. Research has shown very clearly that, for patients who meet certain conditions, which I met, survival is not increased by removal of cancerous lymph nodes. Not only did this surgery probably not benefit me; it may have done harm. My tumor markers were normal before the surgery, but they went way up after surgery and still have not returned to normal now, 12 years later. Surgery can spread cancer. Also, there are some side effects to lymph node removal that I am living with now. I had seen the research before I had the surgery, but all five surgeons were insisting on it anyway, although they could not give me a good reason. Cancer is very frightening, and I just didn't have the strength to stand up to them; I caved.

About five years after my surgery, I asked my breast surgeon why he had insisted on removing my lymph nodes. He said that he probably wouldn't insist on it now, but the research was new at the time, and the standard of care was to be conservative. I can understand that, but it seems to me that he should have explained that to me and let me make the decision.

The next step was chemotherapy, which conventional oncologists recommend when cancer has spread outside the breasts as mine had.

There are tests to assess the potential benefit of chemotherapy, but I was not eligible for those tests because I did not have a breast tumor. Chemotherapy has a lot of potentially very severe side effects, especially for geriatric patients. I wanted to avoid it if possible, but all six medical oncologists that I consulted were recommending it.

By that time, one of the women in my support group told me about her integrative oncologist, and he was quite possibly a lifesaver for me. An integrative oncologist is an MD who is trained both in conventional oncology and in alternative modalities, like nutrition and holistic medicine. He made me feel like someone was on my side. I felt less frightened and less alone. He advised me to go ahead with the chemo, but he gave me a lot of nutritional support that would help with the side effects. We were also both aware of research about fasting to reduce side effects, and I did that too. I also found out on breastcancer.org that there was a chance that the hair loss I would be experiencing could be permanent, not temporary as the medical oncologists had promised. So, I used cold caps that successfully prevented the hair loss. I had a lot of problems after chemo, with vision, hearing, memory, etc., but those things are symptoms of aging as well as of chemo, so I will never know how much I can blame the chemo. I suspect I would have been better off without it, but whether I would feel confident enough to refuse it if I had to do it again, I don't know.

The next step was radiation. The main problem with that is that radiation is a carcinogen. The same friend of a friend who told me about the radiologist with the superior machine warned me against radiation therapy. In 1999, she had a lumpectomy followed by radiation. Then in 2007, she was diagnosed with lung cancer. Her thoracic surgeon told her that the lung cancer was not a metastasis from breast cancer, but rather a new cancer caused by the radiation. She also came down with myelodysplasia, a condition of the bone marrow that can lead to leukemia. She is dead now, from leukemia.

I googled myelodysplasia, and the website of the American Cancer Society said that myelodysplastic syndrome (MSD) as well as several different kinds of leukemia, are all linked to radiation. The risk depends on the amount and type of exposure, and most blood cancers develop after

5 to 9 years. Solid tumors are also linked to radiation, and they usually show up 10 to 15 years after radiation therapy. The only good thing for me is that the risk of all those things decreases with the age of the patient. The American Cancer Society also said that chemotherapy raises the risk of leukemia even more than radiation does. In addition, both chemotherapy and radiation therapy increase the risk of damage to the heart, especially if the radiation is on the left side, which mine would be. None of these things had been disclosed to me by any of the medical oncologists or radiation oncologists.

I asked my integrative oncologist what he thought. He said that if I were his wife or sister, he would want me to have the radiation. So, I met with four radiation oncologists, and the one I chose told me that the radiation would decrease my chances of local recurrence from 30% to 10%; it would increase my chances of lung cancer by 1%; and heart damage by 2%. I had the radiation therapy, which was not as bad as chemo.

The last step was ten years of anti-estrogen hormones, which has been shown to reduce the risk of mortality by as much as 40%. Side effects include high cholesterol, hot flashes, muscle pain, bone thinning, fractures, and joint pain. I had all of them except fractures, but since they are also symptoms of old age, I don't know how much I can blame on the hormones.

Because the main cause of osteoporosis is lack of estrogen, anti-estrogen hormones increase the risk. Therefore, women who take the hormones are also usually treated with bisphosphonates such as Reclast, Fosamax, Actonel, Boniva, Evista, Alendronate, or Zometa to prevent bone loss. My medical oncologist, my endocrinologist and my integrative oncologist all agreed that I should take bisphosphonates to protect my bones.

I looked up bisphosphonates on Wikipedia, which said that they reduced the risk of fractures to the hips by 38% and of fractures to the vertebrae by 62%. However, intravenous bisphosphonates have been associated with osteonecrosis of the jaw (ONJ). I asked my integrative oncologist about ONJ, and he said that the main thing is to avoid dental work while I am on bisphosphonates. I started getting intravenous Zometa twice a year. I had additional DEXA scans after taking hormones and Zometa for two and four years respectively. The bone mineral density (BMD) in my lumbar spine was still normal, and I had a slight improvement in BMD in both hips, although I still had osteopenia.

However, I suffered a serious side effect. In 2014, after three years of anti-estrogen hormones and four doses of intravenous Zometa, I got a toothache and needed an extraction. The oral surgeon didn't want to do it because the surgery would put me at risk for ONJ. He showed me pictures of jaw necrosis, and it is a hideous deformity. You can't predict who will get it, and there is no cure. I asked if I could reduce the risk by stopping the Zometa, and he said no, because the half-life is too long. I looked up what this meant, and I found that bisphosphonates have a half-life of approximately ten years, which means that after ten years, only half of the drug has been eliminated from the body. This means that I can't have any extractions or periodontal surgery or dental implants for the rest of my life without risking ONJ. I knew before I took the Zometa that ONJ was a potential side effect, but I did not know that the percentage was so high or that the side effect would last the rest of my life. Had I been informed of the true risk, I might have made a different decision.

I stopped the Zometa, and got a root canal instead of the extraction, which would only work temporarily because too much tooth structure had been lost. Sometime later, one of my molars became infected and had to come out. This was an emergency, so I had to search quickly for an oral surgeon who I trusted. He did the extraction, but because of my risk of ONJ, which he estimated to be as high as 15%, we just left a hole where the tooth had been. Luckily, it healed eventually and much later I was able to get an implant.

I thought about the fact that millions of post-menopausal women who never had cancer take bisphosphonates because they think it will help to protect their bones. I asked everyone—my dentist, the oral surgeon, and the endodontist—whether all those millions of elderly women are also at risk for ONJ. They all said yes! My risk is higher than theirs because I took a higher dose, but I was told that the statistics indicate that two or three out of every hundred of them will get ONJ if they have a tooth extraction. I doubt that anybody told them about this side effect. Even if ONJ was mentioned, I'll bet that they do not know that they will never be able to have tooth extractions without risking something worse than osteoporosis. Possibly some of them might have opted for the bisphosphonates anyway, but the point is that this should have been their informed decision. I imagine that if patients were really aware of their risk and what it means, sales of bisphosphonates would plummet.

The ten years of hormone therapy marked the end of my cancer treatment. I still get mammograms, MRIs, and ultrasounds, and I see my medical oncologist twice a year, but there will no longer be any treatment unless there is a recurrence. The problem with that is that if there is a recurrence, the cancer will likely no longer be curable. So, we want to prevent a recurrence, and that's where integrative oncology comes in.

Integrative oncologists believe there are two parts to cancer care. The first part is the same thing that conventional oncologists do—some combination of surgery, chemotherapy, radiation, and hormones. Where they differ from conventional oncologists is that they believe there is a second part to cancer care, and that is to alter the "terrain," the body, to make it resistant to cancer. Most of us have cancer cells in our bodies. The issue is whether they remain dormant or grow, and that may be determined by our terrain.

The terrain is affected by five main things that we can control: diet, exercise, supplements, stress, and environmental carcinogens. In order to maximize my chances of staying in remission, I had to change my entire lifestyle. I had to give up meat and dairy, although I can eat fish, and I had to go organic. I take massive amounts of supplements. Environmental carcinogens are in pretty much everything, including food, water, air, plastics, kitchenware, personal care products, household cleaning products, lawn and garden products, and textiles. I had to read labels and change out as many of those things as I could. I did it one step at a time, and my compliance will never be perfect, but I do the best I can. I was already doing exercise as well as stress reduction in the form of meditation to control my thoughts and feelings, and cancer gave me another reason to step it up. Every three or four months I have a blood test to measure the factors that are conducive to cancer, and if anything is off, we correct it, mostly with supplements.

I learned so much from my cancer experience and the information benefited me so much, that I didn't want it to go to waste, so I wrote a book called *The Thinking Woman's Guide to Breast Cancer* with a foreword by my integrative oncologist. The first part of the book is about how to make your own medical decisions, and the second part is about lifestyle changes to stay in remission. I did some speaking engagements, including TV and radio, and the book won some literary prizes for non-fiction. One of my friends is a member of the UN Commission on the Status of Women, and she arranged for me to do a presentation for them. These presentations are on my website, TWGbreastcancer.com. There is also a free weekly newsletter and Facebook page with news about breast cancer. The book came out when I was five years into remission, and it was also my 75th birthday. So, I threw a big party to celebrate all three events.

Appearing on TV to discuss my cancer book, 2017

A BIRTHDAY, A MILESTONE, AND A BOOK!

Please join us in celebrating Janet's 75th birthday, 5 years in remission, and publication of

The Thinking Woman's Guide to Breast Cancer!

Sat, February 11th - 2:00pm - 5:00pm
UCLA Faculty Center - (Closest parking is **Lot 2**)
480 Charles E Young Dr East
Los Angeles, CA, 90024

Hors d'oeuvres and drinks will be served. You are welcome to bring guests, but please RSVP by Feb. 1st with the number.

In lieu of gifts, Janet requests that everyone buy *The Thinking Woman's Guide to Breast Cancer* on Amazon, write a review, and pass the book on to someone affected by cancer.

My evite

Annie, Roya, me, and Nina at my party

With B.J.

Me, Mike, Mateo, Melody, Jane and Tommy with Santa and Mrs. Claus at Santa's Village, 2023

Chapter 8

CONCLUSION

"Participate joyfully in the sorrows of the world. We cannot cure the world of sorrows, but we can choose to live in joy."

– Joseph Campbell

Breast cancer made me change my lifestyle. But I discovered that I also needed to change my friends. With the increased political polarization in the US, it started bothering me that many of them had views that were completely shaped by corporate media. They would believe anything that appeared in *The New York Times* or on CNN; they were not critical thinkers. Even their views on breast cancer were completely conventional, and I was finding it hard to talk with them. When they said things that seemed wrong to me, I had to decide whether to make an issue of it or just shut up and let it go, because it seemed to me that they weren't interested in what I thought. Or I could just make small talk and stay away from many topics that interested me. I finally decided that rather than live with frustration or resentment, I needed to make new friends.

I described my problem to my hairdresser. She is no ordinary hairdresser; she had created an eco-salon free of the usual carcinogens, which is the reason I went there. She is also an accomplished artist with some of her work in the Smithsonian. She invited me to a gathering of interesting women who had various charities, and she asked me to pick up another friend of hers, who operated an environmental charity. We talked in the car, and that person invited me to other events. I connected with her friend group, and the ball started rolling.

I decided I wanted to do something about Americans' lack of critical thinking, so I started another website and another newsletter with a progressive political focus. Some people really appreciated what I was doing, but some of my older group of friends, those who needed it most, didn't even read it.

Every month my newsletter would feature a person and a charity who were doing something to make the world better. I published that newsletter for seven years, so there were a lot of people featured, and it gave me the opportunity to connect with people who were doing important things.

I have a lot of affection for my old friends, and I still maintain those connections, but I spend less time with them and more time with the friends who stimulate me and help me grow. With them, I feel seen, heard, understood, and appreciated.

Looking back over my life, I think I was extraordinarily lucky. In 1962, peyote handed me the key to a good life, so I didn't have to learn all my lessons the hard way. I still had to do the work, but it gave me a head start. And, unlike my mother, I was able to create a life that feels meaningful and happy.

But it wasn't only when I did the work that things turned out well; some things worked to my benefit without any effort from me. For example, my problem with alcohol cured itself. My father's fourth wife having her stroke when she did saved my family relationships. Stepping out of my comfort zone required taking risks, and all those risks worked out fine. Despite having some serious diseases, I arrived in my 80s in pretty good physical and mental health. It seems to me that if the chances of things going in a direction that benefited me were only 50/50, I would not have done as well as I have. I am not a religious person, so I don't want to use a word like blessed, but it does seem to me that something was working in my favor. I want to think that's true for everyone, but when I think about people born in poverty or in war zones, I don't know.

So, what does my future hold? I don't feel finished. I think I have other projects in store. I have learned to trust that my inner guidance will tell me what to do next. Or, as Joseph Campbell would have said, a call comes, and my job is to find the courage to answer it. Meanwhile, I monitor my thoughts and feelings every day, to make sure that the reality I am creating for myself is the one I want.

I have finally come more or less to terms with death. I have no way to know whether anything in my consciousness will survive. But if I am in my right mind when death occurs, I plan to focus on love and trust as I go through the process, in hopes I can create that reality too.

In Samoa, 2023

Thanksgiving toast with the grandkids, 2023

Top row:
Mike, Tommy, Kristina, Jane

Bottom row: Brooke and Melody, me, Ashley and Mateo at Lake Arrowhead, 2023

Hiking in Santa Monica mountains with Tommy, 2022

In the Guadalupe Valley (wine country), Baja California

Mi cuerpo es mio
Mon corps, mon choix
Mein körper gehört mir
Meri zindagi, meri marzi
Mera sharir mera hai
My Body My Choice
I CANNOT BELIEVE I STILL HAVE TO PROTEST THIS SH*T
#Womenforchange

Protesting for progressive causes

www.ingramcontent.com/pod-product-compliance
Ingram Content Group UK Ltd.
Pitfield, Milton Keynes, MK11 3LW, UK
UKHW060101300726
14090UKWH00003B/336

* 9 7 8 0 9 9 7 6 6 1 9 3 4 *